PENGUIN BOOKS

Breaking Even: Divorce, Your Children and You

Jacqueline Burgoyne was born in Worcester in 1944. After her mother's death when she was eight she was cared for by her father and sister until she went to boarding school at the age of fourteen. She was educated at Clifton High School and at Sheffield University where she read sociology. She became a socialist at the age of sixteen as a result of reading Richard Hoggart's *The Uses of Literacy* and her Christian beliefs and commitment to feminism also stem from this period.

After training as a teacher she had a variety of teaching jobs and she has worked at Sheffield City Polytechnic since 1970. Her academic curiosity about couple relationships was first aroused through a study of step-families which she completed with David Clark. She is now working on a study of un-married couples with a grant from the Social Science Research Council. She is a member of the Research Advisory Board of the National Marriage Guidance Council and writes, lectures and broadcasts regularly on marriage and family matters.

A working life spent balancing the competing demands of teaching, research and Polytechnic bureaucracy is sand-wiched between playing squash, running, doing nothing, cooking – Chinese cuisine is her current preoccupation – and gardening.

JACQUELINE BURGOYNE

Breaking Even
Divorce, Your Children and You

PENGUIN BOOKS

For Maureen,
Whose daily, joyous friendship sustained me
while this book was being written

Penguin Books Ltd, Harmondsworth, Middlesex, England
Penguin Books, 40 West 23rd Street, New York, New York 10010, U.S.A.
Penguin Books Australia Ltd, Ringwood, Victoria, Australia
Penguin Books Canada Ltd, 2801 John Street, Markham, Ontario, Canada L3R 1B4
Penguin Books (N.Z.) Ltd, 182–190 Wairau Road, Auckland 10, New Zealand

First published 1984

Made and printed in Great Britain by
Cox & Wyman Ltd, Reading
Filmset in Monophoto Times by
Northumberland Press Ltd, Gateshead, Tyne and Wear

CONTENTS

INTRODUCTION

In the last ten years the divorce rate in Britain has risen dramatically; most people have experienced the effects of a break-up either at first hand or through a member of their family, a friend or a neighbour.

Compared with earlier generations we may seem startlingly nonchalant about divorce: innumerable television sit-coms and domestic dramas rely on family conflict and marriage break-up for their humour and plot; television documentary programmes explain and analyse. But divorce takes on a very different meaning when we have to come to terms with the possibility that our own marriage is in danger.

This book is written primarily for people who are facing this problem as a personal reality, although I hope it will also be read by those who want to help a friend or member of their family in such circumstances. I have also had in mind those whose jobs bring them into contact with people in the throes of separation and divorce. There are now several excellent and helpful books covering many of the legal, bureaucratic and welfare problems faced by separating couples (see Recommended Reading, Appendix 2) and I do not want to add to these. In a way, this is my side of the long and sometimes painful conversations we might have if we were to talk personally about it. At times you will undoubtedly disagree with what is said, but if what I have written makes you think and helps you to find ways of making sense of your experiences as you talk to your partner, your children, family and friends, and also, if necessary, to doctors, social workers and solicitors, it will have achieved its purpose.

As a social scientist, I became interested in divorce almost by accident some years ago when I embarked on a study of step-families. When I first began to plan the research, I decided, rather airily, that we would not need to pay overmuch attention to what had happened to our couples before they met their present partners. However, when David Clark, who worked with me, had his first informal discussions with the couples in our study, we began to see how closely their present circumstances, their hopes and fears for partnerships and family life in the future were shaped by the past, in particular their experiences of broken marriages, separations and divorce. Our full report of this study will be found in *Making a Go of It; a study of step-families in Sheffield* to be published by Routledge & Kegan Paul in the summer of 1984. Many of the ideas in this book spring from our attempts to understand and share their experiences. I would like to record here my gratitude to Sheffield City Polytechnic and to the Social Science Research Council who funded this research and to all the couples who took part, as well as to David who carried out the interviews so sensitively and shared in analysing the data.

In 1981, I was asked by the BBC to act as a consultant for a series of radio programmes about how divorce affects children, entitled 'What are We Doing to the Children?'; this book started life as a short booklet accompanying the series. I shall always be grateful to Sarah Rowlands, the producer, and Jenni Mills, the presenter, for their help. I have frequently quoted from the taped interview material which Jenni collected for the programmes, as well as from the Sheffield remarriage study.

While writing, I have been constantly aware of many other people's experiences of splitting up – friends, chance acquaintances – and of media versions of the private stories of public figures. There is indeed, as several from our remarriage sample commented, 'a lot of it about', and I am indebted to all those who have shared their experiences with me. In a different, but equally significant way I owe a good deal to Diana Cosham for responding so magnificently to the challenge of typing the messy, hand-written chapters I pushed in her direction and to Brenda Chatterton for preparing the appendices.

This book is written with the conviction that, although such events will always cause pain, sometimes more than we imagine possible, and at first will signify only loss and failure, this is not always or inevitably so. Such experiences evoke our strongest and most basic emotions and, while some are selfish and destructive, the persistence, courage and open honesty I have seen exercised by many of those living through this fundamental change in their lives, continues to give me hope.

JB
February 1983

CHAPTER 1

Thinking about Splitting Up

Despite the idealistic images of 'married bliss' and 'perfect partnership' portrayed on television and in magazines, it is probably true that most couples find their marriage a source of unhappiness, conflict or dissatisfaction at some time. People expect a great deal from their home, family and personal relationships, so that conflicts or misunderstandings in this area of their lives usually matter much more than, for example, difficulties at work. However, despite the fact that it is now much easier to get a divorce than it was ten years ago, the majority of married couples still *do not* divorce and those who do eventually decide to split up often go through long periods of stress, indecision and uncertainty before making the final break. When David Clark and I began to listen to many of the accounts offered by the remarried couples in our study, we often found ourselves asking the same question as two Californian researchers, Wallerstein and Kelly, who describe how, 'as the adults talked with us – they spoke with intensity and sincerity, many out of a deep well of tragic feeling, long-lasting loneliness and emotional and sexual deprivation – the question that inevitably formed in our minds about their plight was, "What took you so long?"'[1]

In general, there is little evidence to suggest that the decision to separate is taken lightly, especially when children are involved, although the explanation offered to outsiders may seem glib and insubstantial. As anyone who has ever been directly involved knows, there is usually much more behind statements such as '(s)he's gone off with a colleague' than is disclosed to acquaintances or public officials. Public myths about separation and divorce abound, but few do justice to the private misery experienced by

11

individuals seeking a resolution to the problems of an unhappy partnership.

The landmarks of the dismal journey from first doubts and disappointments to final separation are varied. At one extreme, couples discuss the possibility of splitting up regularly and seriously for a long time before they actually do so, while other marriages end quite abruptly when one partner leaves apparently without warning, to the intense shock and surprise of the partner left behind. Between these extremes, many couples describe how they have slowly grown apart, managing their conflicts by living increasingly separate lives, avoiding painful issues and often hoping that somehow 'things will improve', until eventually some change in their lives causes them to reassess their marriage more fundamentally.

TURNING POINTS

When you talk to people who have been divorced or who have begun to face the problems in their marriage directly, they often focus on a particular period or incident. This may be described years later with exceptional, painful vividness, demonstrating their anger, resentment or sense of failure. It is seen afterwards as some sort of turning point. For example, Mrs Worthing described how her first husband had been violent even before they were married:

> ... even when I were courting, he'd lashed out at me ... but it got worse as he got married 'cos he hit me when I were first carrying Sarah, that's the first one, and I knew then ... I mean, a few months pregnant and he was hitting me ... I sort of had it in the back of my mind all the time that one day I would have to leave him.

During a period in hospital following a miscarriage, Mrs Smithson began to reassess her life:

> I were in hospital a few weeks and just laid there and I just thought there must be something better ... I just did nothing in that ten years as I lived with them but sit in t'house. I just brought three children up, which I don't regret. I wouldn't be without them.

So you made your decision quite quickly then to leave your husband?

Yes, it were because I hadn't thought about it before then. I just sat back and relaxed ... it were just like flashes, you know, in fact me mum can't get over it, she says how I altered.

This turning point may occur at any time, but the anger, conflict and resentments have often built up over a considerable period until one or other partner can bear them no longer.

TWO MARRIAGES

It may sound very obvious but we often forget that inside every marriage there are really *two* marriages, the husband's and the wife's. Even in normal circumstances they may see their partnership very differently because of the differing expectations men and women have of marriage generally. While home and family life complement and provide a refuge from the world of work and careers for men, many women still grow up believing in marriage and motherhood as a career in itself and may, in fact, become permanently trapped within their marriage because of their economic dependence on their husbands. Thus, the quality of their married relationship may mean more to such women, who have more invested in it, than to their husbands, who have other projects on which they can focus their attention when their home life is fraught.

Differences in a husband's and wife's perceptions of their marriage may increase over time, especially if they rarely talk about their feelings together. For example, they may *both* feel that they are the ones making all the sacrifices and concessions; both are dissatisfied, believing that their partner is unaware of all they are doing to make their marriage work. The partners may have completely different views about how their relationship is working out – what is tolerable or even satisfactory for one may be increasingly unbearable for their mate. In such circumstances, the fact that one partner wishes to end the marriage may come as a complete shock to the other, who had not thought there was anything seriously

13

amiss. Separations by mutual agreement are relatively unusual, as cracks in a marriage are often recognized at first by one partner only. However, when couples discuss their relationship as they try to decide what to do, they may begin to see their partner's point of view more clearly so that, even if they do split up, they are both able to make sense of what has happened to them. This is particularly important if they have children and will have a continuing relationship as parents. There is some evidence that continued disputes over money and children are more likely to occur when one partner cannot accept that the marriage is over.[2]

PROBLEMS BUILD UP

EARLY DAYS

Some couples find their marriages difficult from the very beginning. Couples who leave home for the first time when they get married, or who build up their hopes of married life from the somewhat idealized pictures of romantic fiction and advertising, often find the first months of marriage much more of a strain than they had expected. The period of activity and excitement before a wedding is frequently followed by a sense of anticlimax after it.[3] Even in ideal circumstances, with secure jobs and a place of their own, many young couples who have never lived away from home before have few resources to deal with the inevitable adjustments and disappointments as they embark on domestic life together. If they are living with in-laws or were already expecting a baby when they married, their problems are compounded. Many of the divorcees in the Sheffield remarriage study felt they had married too young. They still spoke many years later of the resentment they felt at 'having to' get married, so that, while they may have made the best of things at the time, when their marriage began to deteriorate all their old resentments resurfaced. They described the abrupt loss of freedom and independence that marriage and imminent parenthood had brought in its train. In such circumstances, becoming parents placed a strain on their relationship from which they felt it had never really recovered. It was significant that when we asked the parents in our study what sort of advice about marriage they might give to their children, nearly all of them referred to the dangers of getting married too young.

HAVING AND BRINGING UP CHILDREN

Popular mythology dictates that 'children make a marriage', but, if a wide range of research evidence is to be believed, the reverse is true. Research of various kinds suggests that parents are less satisfied with many aspects of their partnership than they were before they had children.[4] In particular they felt less close to their partner than they had been before.

Having children seems to follow quite naturally and inevitably from getting married; indeed, it is couples who postpone or decide not to have any children who have to justify their decision. Many couples are ill-prepared for the impact parenthood will have upon their lives. Families today are smaller and most live in greater isolation than was common two generations ago, so that many young couples have little sustained contact with small children before their own children arrive. Although having children affects both partners, its consequences for women are much more dramatic. Most women leave paid work and become full-time housewives until their youngest child starts school. Although fathers are more involved in bringing up children than they would have been a generation or so ago, mothers are still regarded as being primarily responsible for the day-to-day care of children and take most of the credit or blame for how they eventually turn out.

After the arrival of children, a husband's and wife's experience of daily life alters dramatically. While he continues in paid work, now more highly motivated to keep his job and improve his earnings because of his family responsibilities, she is increasingly pre-occupied with the routines, responsibilities and anxieties of daily child care. This distinction is sometimes the first stage in a process of growing apart which eventually leads to couples splitting up.

Women who stay at home to look after children under five are subject to a good deal of stress and they are more likely than other groups of adults to be depressed and to be prescribed tranquil-lizers.[5] In a recent survey, mothers with small children who were

15

asked what they thought of as a special treat most frequently answered in terms of getting away from the children for a while. By contrast, a similar proportion of men in the same age group said their idea of a treat was being *with* their children.[6] The pressures of those years are graphically described by one of the women in the Sheffield study:

> I wanted something out of life; as it was, I was getting nothing out of life and that was it ... You read about people that are prisoners in their own home and I was, I were lonely, even though I'd got the kids. OK, it's great having your kids ... I love them, but you *need* adult conversation as well, you need something else, everybody does.

For Mrs Parkes, this led to the break-up of her first marriage:

> I'm a person in me own right now, whereas before, I wasn't. I was just a wife and mother and that was it. You've got to have something else in life or you just simply go round the twist and I think this is what *did* break up our marriage, it was like living in a prison constantly ...

GROWING APART

Romantic fiction usually portrays the wedding as the climax to a story of misunderstanding and difficulty transcended; from there on the couple are destined to live 'happily ever after'. This rosy picture of unclouded bliss does nothing to alert us to the considerable changes which, even in the normal course of events, will be experienced by married individuals during a partnership which might last for fifty years. Although we observe the milestones of the physical, intellectual and emotional development of children and adolescents very closely, we tend to assume that growth and change are over once we reach 'adulthood'. But some young couples in their early twenties seem so seriously committed to domestic life and home-making that they have become fossilized into premature middle-age, while older couples may be putting their energies into recapturing an almost lost youth.

Our fixed notions of appropriate behaviour for people of different ages have been greatly undermined in the past ten years or so. 'Normal' career patterns in work and in family life have been challenged in a number of ways. For example, though progress has been dreadfully slow, women have begun to make their mark in many occupations, challenging the assumption that an unbroken record of service to their families and others is the only kind of acceptable career pattern for them. High unemployment rates mean that an unbroken work career is no longer to be taken for granted by men either, and changes in technology have necessitated considerable job mobility. Similarly, the dramatic rise in the divorce rate has meant that the marriage patterns of any given age group are much more diverse than in the past. For example, any group of friends in their mid-thirties meeting today will include men and women who have never been married, married and cohabiting couples without children, and married, divorced and remarried parents. Such diversity subtly alters our awareness, alerting us to new alternatives. Many people in their thirties and forties now feel, and present themselves as, younger than their parents would have done at the same age. As a result, they are more sensitive to the possibilities of change and the potential for personal growth in adult life.

Individual growth and change place their own strain on married partnerships as the potential and the pace of change may not be the same. It is often at the time when women are most deeply immersed in home and child care that their husbands are making their way in the world of work. Initially united in a joint project of making a home and creating a family together, they may begin to ask 'what's next?' at different times or to come up with different answers.

Mr Thornleigh, a keen railway enthusiast, could not get his first wife to share his hobby with him:

> All she was bothered about was shopping and her mother's ... She was quite happy to stop at home and watch television ... towards the end I got a car, so I says 'come on, let's go out for the day'. 'Oh no, I don't feel like it, but you go and take the kids.' So I did. So, the last three or four years, it was just me and the kids that went out and she stopped at home.

Mr Pelham described how

> ... the marriage went quite well initially. We had a new house
> and you've got things to do ... your life is reasonably full. Then
> the boredom factor doesn't enter into it. When you've got
> established, when your house is organized, when your garden's
> done, when everything's organized, then you start looking for
> something else and you either turn to your wife or husband,
> whatever, or you turn to outside interests, sport, booze or
> whatever ...

When she looked back, a year after her marriage ended, one of the
mothers in the radio series concluded:

> I suppose you could say it hasn't been a happy marriage right
> from the beginning, but I must admit I did try to work very hard
> at it, and I suppose in a way he did too, but then I realized, when
> the decorating had come to an end and things were getting
> straight in the house, that there wasn't really much between us.

'SURELY THERE MUST BE MORE TO MARRIAGE THAN THIS?'

External events, both the routine, predictable happenings of our
lives and the unexpected surprises, often precipitate more subtle
changes as we gradually alter our perceptions of ourselves, our goals
and ambitions, and re-evaluate partnerships and family life. Evans
and Bartolomé studied how a group of senior managers balanced
work and family life. They found that men in their twenties, who
are simultaneously involved in setting up three 'careers', in business, as husbands and as fathers, concentrate initially on their work
careers. Later, when more established at work, they turn their
attention to home and family and may, at this stage, begin to want
more from their marriage. By contrast, other men become intensely
involved in leisure activities as they reach a plateau in their work
careers, spending even less time at home. Others, including women
who return to take up new careers after they have reared children,
find much more absorbing work and careers after several false
starts, and begin to immerse themselves in work in their thirties,
developing interests, confidence and a sense of identity which may
surprise and disturb their partner, who begins to feel left behind.

Such crises and changes are very common and many couples recognize and deal with them as they painfully renegotiate their relationship. One forty-year-old wife of a manager told the researchers:

> Every marriage goes through a bad patch. And we did a few years back ... I think we just simply stopped communicating for a number of years ... I forgot what he was like really. And then we started to have terrible rows. We gradually started communicating again. It was either that or we would have split up ... But we didn't like each other very much for a year or so. We'd drink too much and yell at each other. I thought it was all me at the time, but I look back on it and part of it was him. He's a very controlled person. He tended to retreat into himself or leave the house if I got angry about something ... But gradually he started being more open, and we began talking again. Really talking.[7]

Others learn to withdraw in order to avoid painful conflicts and disagreements, and eventually realize that their marriage is bringing little happiness. Another of the managers in Evans and Bartolomé's study said:

> With regard to my wife, I think it is my fault. I feel distant and detached. We don't talk much together. I hide behind my shell, and I think she does the same. She feels that there is something wrong so she withdraws. It isn't worth saying anything. I'll tell you frankly, what concerns me is that, if I let it go on like that, we'll land up in a state of total indifference to each other. It's up to me. Things drift on and I don't know whether to accept this or do something about it.[8]

DOING SOMETHING ABOUT IT

Although most married people find themselves asking the question 'is this all there is?' at some point in their lives, they do not necessarily take any action either to improve or to end their marriage. Some of those who do may be driven to do so by the extremity of their circumstances. Many of the women we spoke to in Sheffield who had suffered in very violent marriages described how other

19

people had helped them to make up their mind about leaving. When they saw their suffering through someone else's eyes, they realized they must make a decision. If they came into contact with people who could give them practical help and advice, this too helped to speed things up. The miseries of unhappy marriages, whether as obvious and extreme as persistent violence or as subtle and destructive as nagging and continuous rejection, tend to be endured in secret, so that talking to someone else about the problem is itself a significant step.

In less extreme circumstances, meeting someone new precipitates the end of many marriages where partners have grown apart over a long period. Some of the people in the Sheffield study described how they had begun, with varying degrees of conscious purpose, to search for potential new partners, while others characterized their new relationship as completely unsought and unexpected. In the first instance, for example, women who have returned to work after their youngest child starts school, may consciously recognize they are on the lookout for a new partner when they begin to go out on their own. Mrs Thornleigh speaks:

> I started going out with the girls from work and I suppose it's the same old story . . . out with the girls, only dancing you know, once or twice a week. I'd got my own money 'cos I was working, I'd found my independence and that was the end.

Mrs Parkes took a job as a barmaid and, as a result, met her second husband. This relationship gave her, as she put it, 'the opportunity I'd been looking for, to leave my husband'. Others fall in love apparently out of the blue, aware only of a dimly recognized loneliness and dissatisfaction with their marriage which had made them more vulnerable. Mrs Dunwell said:

> I must have known for four years previously that it wasn't working, it wasn't right, it wasn't what I wanted. I think you give out feelings and vibrations to other people . . . At parties and things, I always found that I would attract other fellas, not particularly because I thought I was trying to flirt with them or anything – no more than you would at an ordinary party anyway . . . I thought this was really strange. Then looking back, it's because I think I was unhappy and that you need someone else

... you know you're giving out all these vibes that you need someone to lean on and talk to.

Now that divorce is much more common, most parties and social events, offices and workplaces, include divorcees as well as men and women in the throes of separation or consciously considering leaving their partners. It is now more difficult to categorize the availability of people we meet and complex declarations must be made as people become acquainted. As they exchange experiences, glad of the opportunity to share some of the pain, a relationship between two people may develop very quickly, even before they have had time to work out how it might affect their marriages. For example, many men in their late thirties and early forties emerge from a period in their lives when they have devoted most of their energies to building a successful career, only to discover that they no longer have much in common with their wives, who have, in turn, built separate lives for themselves while their husbands were absorbed in their careers. Suddenly these men have time to spare, they want to build up leisure interests to counterbalance work and, above all, they want someone to talk to. In general, most men find it easier to talk personally to women, and they seek out someone they know at work or through a leisure pursuit, someone who understands the kind of person they have become during their work-filled twenties and thirties and with whom they can share their present interests and preoccupations. When they complain, 'my wife doesn't understand me', they are not necessarily considering exchanging one wife for another, but they fall in love and suddenly their marriage is called into question. By the same token, women in their thirties who return to work or embark on further study begin to see themselves differently, gaining confidence through the discovery that they are still attractive to men. When they meet someone who takes their new identity seriously, who encourages their new projects, they feel appreciated as an individual rather than simply as a wife and mother.

Unless both partners embark on new relationships at about the same time, there are two very distinctive sides to this kind of story. For many of the divorcees in the Sheffield study the discovery, sometimes completely unexpected, that their partner was having an affair precipitated a sequence of confrontations, recriminations and changes which eventually led to divorce. Some communicated their sense of complete surprise very clearly. Mrs Hurst, whose first husband was a bus driver, described how:

> ... only just by accident I found a blonde hair on his jacket and then I said to one of the neighbours, 'I think he's got another woman.' She says, 'Don't be silly,' so I went round to see his mate and asked, 'Do you know if Charlie's got someone else in the Transport?' He says 'No, not to my knowledge,' so he asked him and he (her husband) come and said he had and that he wanted to leave me for her.

Barbara first discovered her husband was having an affair when she found a present from his girlfriend in the glove compartment of his car. Looking back, she realized he had been

> ... very upset and he was worrying about something, and I kept asking him what was wrong and he wouldn't tell me. He was out quite a lot but he was working as a minicab driver on a part-time basis and it was quite easy to come in at one o'clock, two o'clock in the morning without me realizing.

Some people decide to do nothing about such discoveries; for a variety of reasons they are prepared to accept their partner's infidelities. They may hope for a reconciliation when the affair is over, or they may not wish to alter their domestic arrangements or subject their children to the disruption of separation and divorce. Married people who are having an affair tend to experience the greatest stress while they are making up their minds what to do. Typically they leave home, perhaps to set up home with their new partner, and then return for a time in a final desperate effort to make their marriage work. In the radio programmes, Mel and Marge described how they first met and fell in love. Mel left home at the time he first told Sue, his wife, about Marge. He stayed one night at a local Y M C A, then moved in with Marge before going to live with his mother. He returned to his wife after the birth of their second child. This 'to-ing and fro-ing stage' as Marge graphically described it, lasted until he eventually reached a final decision.

What was the point at which you took the final decision?

I don't really know. It was the going backwards and forwards. I came to realize that it was really the wrong thing to do and I had to make an absolute decision, a final decision, and I decided it had to be to go and live with Marge and wait for a divorce and get married.

Even if it meant leaving your children?

Yes, even if it meant leaving the children. You have to decide sooner or later who you love more and who you want to spend your life with.

STAYING TOGETHER FOR THE SAKE OF THE CHILDREN

The decision to split up, whether it is eventually made jointly or is pressed upon an unwilling husband or wife who still wants their marriage to continue, is always more difficult if there are children involved. Indeed, the one who is left behind, and who doesn't want the marriage to end, frequently tries to persuade their partner to stay, 'if only for the sake of the children'. Couples who are going through marriage difficulties often ask advisers, doctors, social workers and teachers and so on, what would be best for their children in such circumstances. In the past, public opinion, supported by expert knowledge of various kinds, was clear. As a result, many parents endured joyless marriages at least until their children left home, although by that time it was usually too late, for the wife at least, to find a new partner and a more rewarding relationship. Today, opinion is more divided and there is no conclusive research evidence. Indeed, there is surprisingly little research of any kind about how divorce affects children, and the prescriptions of those who work with the children of unhappy marriages differ greatly. In any event, we cannot rely on other people, whatever their qualifications, to make our personal decisions for us. What is far more important is that *both* parents try to work out what is best for their children, even when this means facing up to ending their marriage.

As I researched the background for the radio programmes, I

became increasingly aware that the most damaging aspects of separation and divorce for the children are probably the quarrelling, conflict and uncertainty which characterize the period when the parents are deciding whether to split up or not. If 'staying together for the sake of the children' means continuing the quarrels or the cold, loveless indifference which originally precipitated the crisis in the marriage, then there is little point in staying together under one roof for the sake of appearances. A woman writing to the *Guardian*, looking back ten years later on her experiences of her parents' attempts to stay together, concluded:

> On balance I think it would have been better if my parents had split up earlier and been more honest with us ... My parents had intended to stay together until the three children had left home – that my mother finally left abruptly just at the build-up to my A-levels (I was the youngest) reflects the almost intolerable strain we had all been living under for far too long ...
>
> It is very hard to spend most of your childhood and teens in a house where you can't even remember seeing your parents touch or kiss one another and where their separate bedrooms are a constant source of embarrassment when friends come to stay. It is very hard never to be told openly that the marriage is failing when you can sense it all around you and eventually hear 'second-hand' from so-called friends what your parents kept from you 'in your best interests'.[9]

Some parents do find that they can renegotiate their relationship in a way which meets more of each other's needs. If this reduces conflict there may be no need to split up. The couples most likely to benefit from the kind of help provided by marriage counselling agencies (see Appendix 1) are those who are finding it difficult to talk together about their relationship, but who would *both* like to try and improve things. In these circumstances, parents have to balance their own need for a fulfilling partnership and personal life with their responsibilities towards their children.

Some critics of trends in contemporary society argue that we have become too preoccupied with our own need for personal fulfilment at the expense of wider family and community responsibilities. Nevertheless, we still regard divorce as a much more serious matter if it involves children because of the deep-seated beliefs we hold about parental obligations. The most damning criticism we can make of any parent is that (s)he gives up or drops out before the responsibilities of parenthood are fulfilled. While the terms 'ex-husband' and 'ex-wife' have now been absorbed into our social vocabulary, we do not speak of 'ex-sons' or 'ex-daughters' even though, as we shall see in Chapter 3, children may lose touch completely with their non-custodial parents. One of the most difficult things that has to be faced by parents who are contemplating separation is the way it will affect their children, altering and possibly diminishing their relationship with them. Unfortunately, most people's impressions of being a divorced parent are entirely negative. Newspaper and television coverage of such problems focuses on the most extreme situations, for example, on the so-called 'tug-of-love' cases or court reports of custody or access disputes. Our attention is more frequently drawn to the unusual problems, wherever they occur, than to the many divorced parents who quietly and responsibly work at their new relationships.

It is worth pointing out that the pursuit of personal goals and the meeting of wider family responsibilities are not necessarily mutually exclusive alternatives; rather, the reverse may be true. People who derive a strong sense of their own worth from their adult investments and relationships may offer more to their children than those who, as they sometimes put it, 'live only for their children'. Remaining in a destructive marriage for the sake of the children may, in the end, be the weak solution, even if, at the time, it seems to be a courageous self-sacrifice of personal needs.

It is worth remembering that many divorced parents resolve their outstanding conflicts well enough to continue cooperating as parents. Divorce does not inevitably mark the end for the parent without custody; children may live in a one-parent household but they do not inevitably lose a parent after divorce. The writer A. Alvarez described how he struggled with the decision to leave his wife. When he discussed his fears with a psychotherapist he was told, 'You will not cease to be a father by living apart. You may be more of one.'[10]

HOW CAN WE HELP THE CHILDREN DURING THIS TIME?

One of the few pieces of research on how divorce affects children is Wallerstein and Kelly's much-quoted Californian Study (see Appendix 2). Although it is difficult to assess how generally applicable their findings are, especially outside the United States, many of their conclusions ring true to those of us involved in different ways with children of divorced parents. In particular they suggest a number of factors which help or prevent the children's adjustment to their parents' divorce. These include:

1. the extent to which the parents had been able to resolve and put aside their conflict and anger and make use of the relief from conflict provided by the divorce;
2. the custodial parent's handling of the child(ren) after separation.

For families who have been at war for months, or even years, the separation itself brings relief. Children welcome the end of their parents' conflicts and arguments. Scott, aged seven, returned again and again to his recollections of his parents' dreadful quarrels:

> I didn't really like it, and I kept on saying 'stop it' to them but they kept on arguing and mum kept on telling me off, to go away and that ...
>
> When they kept on arguing I couldn't really play, they were arguing so loud, and I tried to go up in my bedroom and that and try and go away, but they kept on arguing.

Later, when he was asked what he thought about his mum and dad not being together any longer, he replied:

> I think it's much better ... because they don't argue so much now.

Nearly all children of divorced parents would have preferred their parents to stay together and Scott is no exception:

> ... On Saturday I like it 'cos ... I can see my dad and I can see mum as well. I like it very much on Saturdays.

Do you miss your dad?

Well, I always see mum a lot and I wish I saw dad quite a lot as well. But if they lived together and didn't quarrel I'd be much happier.

Scott was very distressed during the period before his parents split up. His behaviour mirrored his mother's own anxieties as she began to suspect her husband was having an affair:

> ... I think I refused to believe that anything was going on. I thought, 'this can't be happening to me' and although I was very upset at the fact that he wasn't spending much time at home, I just refused to believe that there was anything going on, so I just played along although the atmosphere was bad and he'd usually pick the time when I was putting Scott to bed and I'd hear the front door go and he'd be gone – I think it was to avoid a confrontation. Scott noticed it too, because as I was putting him to bed he said, 'Is Daddy going out again?' and I would say, 'No' and the next minute I'd hear the door go. The atmosphere was getting very bad, but I obviously tried to keep things as calm as possible because of Scott.

During this time, she found it very difficult to get Scott to sleep at night, as he was anxious that something might happen while he was upstairs:

> He wouldn't go to bed and go to sleep ... probably the first thing was, 'Can you read me another story, I'm getting lonely up here on my own.' And then the next stage was 'Can you leave the hall light on?' and the next stage a few weeks after that was, 'Can you leave the door open so I can hear the television?' and then it was just continual, 'I want a drink,' and some nights I've been taking him back up to bed at half-past ten, eleven o'clock at night.

In order to avoid the conflicts which took place at mealtimes he refused to eat at the table. His mother eventually realized that both she and her husband, Keith, had begun to pick on him:

> If he spilt anything or said he didn't like his food I went for him, because of the way I was feeling, it was an effort to cook a meal, but it got to the stage when it was easier to just let him play and he did ask that he and I have our meal before Keith

got in from work because he said 'you and I can talk, but you and daddy don't talk'. —

Scott's grandmother described how he 'shut himself off from most things' during this time. On one occasion he broke down completely, and on another was ill with an unexplained high temperature. He was at his grandmother's house when he suddenly wanted to return home. His aunt tried to persuade him to put his jumper back on before they went outside:

> He went absolutely berserk. Slamming doors, banging, kicking her. It was awful. And she cried and I cried and in the end he sort of, how shall I put it, fought himself out and he sat on my lap and sobbed his heart out to me.

Scott's grandmother, Dora, had told the school about his problems at home and one day his head teacher brought him home because he had a high temperature:

> That day he sat in his chair all day. He just wouldn't communicate. He didn't eat or drink anything, he didn't speak for the rest of the day.

He slept that night, but when he got up the next day he went straight to his chair:

> He didn't move and that was when I realized there was something radically wrong. So eventually I very patiently got him dressed. I knew I had to bring him out somehow and get him talking again, and knowing how he loves his teddy bear, my only thought was we'd take Ben for a walk. And I knew he liked pushing my trolley, so I stuffed a cushion in the bottom so Ben could, sort of, stand up and as we walked through the park, every communication was through Ben ... by the time we walked back through the park he was conversing.

Dora concluded:

> Anyone can tell me that a child can't have a nervous breakdown at – what was he? – six. Well I just wouldn't believe them because I saw it with me own eyes. It might have been a minor one, and it didn't last very long, but it was a nervous breakdown.

Scott's stress during this period of indecision was very obvious and his parents, his grandmother and other members of his family were all very worried about him. His reactions highlight two of the greatest difficulties children face at this time. He found the arguments and conflict between his parents intolerable and tried, wherever possible, to withdraw from it but, at the same time, he desperately needed to know what was happening. His mother and grandmother described how, although they tried to make arrangements about the house, deal with solicitors and so on without him knowing, he always worked out what they were planning.

Similarly, Mr Heathcote, awarded custody of his two children after his wife left home, describes how they seemed to be able to sense that something was happening. Their mother often used to stay away at night and they began to creep into his bed at night:

> ... as though the children knew what were going off. In fact, Richard was eight at the time and subsequently it transpired that he often listened in on the telephone extension to his mother talking to her boyfriend ... what the child heard, I don't know, he's never repeated, but it's obviously had a tremendous effect on that child.

When children are worried or distressed, this shows itself in a variety of ways, affected by their age, maturity and how they normally communicate their fears. As well as asking direct questions at embarrassing and inopportune moments, they may demonstrate their concern more indirectly. Sudden changes in behaviour may indicate that they are trying to say something which neither they, nor their parents, can face directly. While some children revert to childish habits long abandoned – wetting the bed, needing a light on at night, being difficult about food – others suddenly seem to grow up, to become almost unnaturally good, trying hard to please their parents in order to hold the family group together.

Some children, whose behaviour remains very much the same at home, start reacting very differently at school, so that their teacher is the first person to be aware of their distress. Scott began to be very aggressive at school, expressing the depression and rage which built up at home. Fortunately, his grandmother decided to talk to

Scott's teacher when he returned to school after a particularly difficult weekend:

> On Monday morning, I was so worried about him going off to school, I thought, well, that poor little lad, what he's been through this weekend, what if someone upsets him at school? That was when I phoned his headmistress and explained things a bit to her and had a long chat over the phone and she was more than pleased I did phone.

Scott, like other children in similar situations, needed help because of his reactions to the emotionally charged atmosphere at home combined with the gathering uncertainty about what would happen next. While adults and children both need continuity in their lives, children live very much more in the present, so that daily domestic routines and rituals are especially important to them. During the periods of crisis which occur when a married couple are openly considering or planning to separate, the ordinary domestic routines of family life are often disrupted in a way which threatens the children's stability and security. Children need some sort of reassurance and explanation if their parents seem unusually irritable or preoccupied, or if they frequently burst into tears or spend long hours closeted behind closed doors together. They are also disturbed by obviously 'adult' conversations with the family or friends that they do not fully understand.

Parents are naturally absorbed with their own needs at such a time and may well be unaware of how easily children, of whatever age, can sense such changes in family atmosphere. If you are ever directly involved, it is worth considering whether the children are really too young to know what is happening. At times of crisis we should listen particularly carefully to the comments and questions of the children involved to get a clearer idea of their particular anxieties, preoccupations and misconceptions. This may sometimes be done by playing a game, drawing pictures together or encouraging a child to speak through the family pet or even a favourite toy. Scott's grandmother helped him talk by asking questions through his favourite teddy, Ben.

Because of their own strong emotions, it may be impossible for parents to talk calmly to their children about what is happening.

If they are afraid of bursting into tears or of being very vindictive about their partner it may be a good idea to ask another trusted adult to try to talk to their children, perhaps a grandparent, an aunt or uncle or their teacher. If there is a good deal of upheaval at home but no definite decisions have yet been made, children need to know that their parents are in control, however tenuously, and that they have not been forgotten.

We are usually told that the more important the decision, the more slowly and carefully it should be made, but this may be difficult for couples considering separation and eventual divorce. If one partner has already reached a decision it is, in a sense, no longer a joint matter, although there will be many other things which will need to be sorted out together afterwards. Couples who take some time to decide, and who have the opportunity to consider and discuss what has happened, are less likely to go on fighting after they split up than those who give each other little opportunity to speak about their disappointments, grievances or feelings of guilt. In a sense they need to give their marriage a decent burial before they can contemplate a different, but continuing, relationship based on their joint parenthood. Although the time taken in making up their minds may be helpful to parents, it is a particularly difficult time for children, especially if they are treated to a series of contradictory promises about the future. It is not unusual for statements like 'Your dad and I have definitely decided to split up – he'll be gone by the end of next week,' to be followed the next day by promises that 'We are going to stay together and we're planning to take you all camping in France in the summer holidays.' Although such dramatic changes in mood are quite natural and normal in the circumstances, they should, if possible, be kept from the children.

The realization that what is happening is making their children unhappy adds immeasurably to some parents' guilt and anxiety at this time, and it is important for them to realize that their children may be reacting most strongly to the uncertainty, insecurity and change in the air. They will not necessarily go on behaving like this once decisions have been made. If parents can reassure their children that they are still loved and that their needs are considered, they will help them to acquire the confidence and resilience necessary to face any changes.

31

CHAPTER 2

Separation and After

These next two chapters make a division which rarely occurs in real life. The material in this chapter deals with the effects of ending a marriage for both partners, and the problems of loss, adjustment and learning to make a fresh start which arise when any couple splits up. Consideration of the special problems of parents is deferred until Chapter 3. This somewhat arbitrary distinction may remind us that it is often necessary to recognize your *own* feelings and needs before you try to face the problems and fulfil the responsibilities which arise because of relationships and commitments to *other* people, including children. In practice, it is hard to make such a distinction. If you are a parent, 'keeping going' means responding to your children's needs as they arise, even when your own problems seem overwhelming. Nevertheless, it is convenient to consider some of the issues separately.

DIFFERENT KINDS OF SEPARATIONS

Separation takes many forms. Some are gradual, planned and anticipated, others sudden and completely unexpected. Although divorce marks the legal end of a marriage, there are no such obvious milestones to mark the ending of the personal, emotional relationship. For most people, the breaking up of their home, as one or both of them moves elsewhere, is a critical stage, especially if they have consciously prepared for separation over a considerable period. Mrs Baker, shocked and hurt when she discovered that her husband had been unfaithful, knew at once that their marriage was over:

If we'd stayed together it would have gone from bad to worse because it was already implanted in me mind and people had already started talking and that was the end of the marriage.

The decision came quickly but they went on living together

from June till the November I moved here. We stayed in the same house, we kept, not appearances up for the children, we told them what was going on. Occasionally I lost me temper with him, I mean, when I was ironing shirts for him to go out with his girlfriend ... but I think now it really did pay off with the children.

On the day she moved into her new house with the children, her husband

moved us in and fixed the gas fire in and plumbed the washer in and then he dropped us off at me mother's for our tea and he says to the kids, 'well I'm off now', they said 'ta-ra' and they knew he was going for good.

Scott's mother, Anne, whom we met in the previous chapter recognized the significance of the moment of separation when, by arrangement, Keith finally moved out of their house. She had been staying with her mother while he found somewhere else to live:

... it was getting impossible at Mum's, all Scott wanted to do was to come home. He said he would go on Thursday, and I said to him, 'Well, about seven o'clock in the evening,' and he said, 'Yes,' and I said, 'As you're about to leave you can phone Mum's and just let the phone ring twice and I'll know you're on your way, that you've gone ...' and Mum took Scott out for a walk and I was just waiting for him to phone which meant he'd gone and I could move back again ... and I was looking at the clock and dead on seven o'clock, the phone rang twice; although I was eager before the phone went to get back up here, as soon as I heard that phone ring twice, I felt that was very final, and I must admit that I sat there and I broke my heart, and wondered whether I'd been doing the right thing and whether things could have been sorted out.

Others who split up over a period of months or even years find it harder to pinpoint a moment of final separation. Two of the men in the Sheffield study described how job transfers helped to conceal the breakdown of their marriages. In Mr Johnson's case

> [my company] wanted me to work in Birmingham on a short secondment for six weeks ... but it spun out for three years in fact and this actually presented an occasion for splitting without appearing to do so.

After Mr Roberts and his wife had discussed splitting up, he went to see his boss:

> We had a southern office ... I had a good boss and he sent me down to London for about nine months ... although we separated officially between us-selves, if she hadn't told any-body, as far as anybody knew I'd just gone down south to work. When I came home at weekends I slept in the back room and that was it.

Housing nearly always plays a critical part in determining when and how a couple actually split up. If they own their own home they must decide whether one of them will stay on there and how the finances will be arranged. This usually takes time and, as we have seen, they may go on living in the same house during this period. If one of them already has somewhere else to go this may precipitate the final break.

Some people have described a bizarre kind of musical chairs which is played when the couples in a chain of extramarital affairs begin to split up: John and Anne are having an affair; once Anne's husband has left home, it is not long before John moves in with her; his wife, Jane, was already seriously involved with another married man; when she is 'free' there is little to stop him moving in and taking John's place ...

Others who have begun to find living together intolerable eventually leave without warning even if they have no alternative accommodation. Some people may return to their parents' house for a short time, although this has obvious disadvantages. Mrs Turner's parents welcomed her back but

> I think after having a home of your own, being a reasonably free

agent ... I decided that, as well as I got on with my parents, I couldn't stay there permanently ... and I think I were only there about two months when a friend of mine who I used to go to school with, contacted me and she said she'd got a cottage which she needed someone to share the expenses with.

Similarly, Mr Brown felt that it was inappropriate for his parents to be burdened with his troubles:

> I were made more than welcome at me mother's ... but I felt a bit sorry for me parents ... why should they have my troubles ... they've brought their family up and got them off their hands ... so I were glad when I met Jean [his second wife].

ILLNESS AND STRESS

Many divorced people experience serious and prolonged ill-health at some time during the period between the first hints of serious problems and the time when they feel they are finally over the worst. For those who see themselves as taking the initiative, whose hopes and intentions are directing them towards ending their marriage, the stress tends to be greatest while they are still making up their minds. They may have difficulty eating or sleeping normally and find themselves smoking and drinking more than usual. During this period of indecision many people find it difficult or impossible to work properly. Mr Moseley, one of the divorcees in the Sheffield study who took a long time deciding whether to leave his wife, told us how he

> lost ... I don't know ... about two stone in weight. I couldn't sleep very well and I didn't really feel like eating at times ... I found it difficult to concentrate ... I had a lot of headaches. Obviously I got further behind with me paperwork, so I had to bring it home but it didn't always seem to work.

Like many women in her situation, Mrs Chapman suffered greatly with her nerves and was given tranquillizers by her doctor:

> ... in fact I never came off nerve pills at all for about two years ... I was too frightened to go out and fetch them for myself and

35

I used to send my eldest daughter up to the doctor's ... I was thinking about it all the time, you know, trying to plan out what I were going to do and how it would turn out, whether I would get custody of the children and the house ... I was trying to make me mind up, to push myself to go in for a divorce ... it were, like, at the back of me mind all the time.

Mrs Thornleigh also took 'all sorts of silly tablets' during the time when she was trying to decide what to do about the affair she was having with her, now, second husband. In such circumstances making a decision, whatever its consequences, brings some measure of relief:

... it seemed, as if, as though ... everything had been lifted off my shoulders and I was glad that it was all over ... the last couple of years had been really traumatic ... even though it was basically my fault, afterwards, after it was all over, I felt a lot better.

By contrast, those who see themselves as the passive victims of their partner's actions and decisions experience the greatest stress in the period after they are left alone trying to rebuild their lives; angry and depressed, they lack the energy and confidence necessary to make a fresh start. If their partner departs suddenly and completely unexpectedly, feelings of shock and panic may persist for a long time. Mrs Hurst was ill for two years after her first husband left her:

I was very nervous, frightened of being in the house on me own at night ... I tended to be awake most nights and I had an accident at home when I got me hand in the wringer and I had to go to hospital. When I went to the hospital they said that I'd bottled me feelings up and it all came out after that wringer incident and I went hysterical and they thought they'd have to keep me in ... they said it was with me husband leaving me and the shock coming out afterwards.

MOURNING FOR A LOST PARTNER

When members of our family, friends or acquaintances tell us of the end of their marriage, there is often a certain ambiguity in our response. We do not always know how to react because it is difficult to assess *their* feelings. An abrupt and unexpected departure plainly provokes sympathy, support and condolences for the 'injured' innocent party who did not, apparently, want their marriage to end, but what do we say to someone who announces their separation from a violent, alcoholic or bad-tempered, overbearing or nagging partner? While we may share someone's joy in finding a potential new partner with whom they obviously have much more in common, it is impossible to ignore the past. Our contradictory responses to such announcements mirror the conflicting feelings experienced at the time by everyone involved.

Deserted partners mourn the passing of marriage, which they did not want to end, as well as grieving for their departed spouse. In such circumstances they are likely to go on believing that their partner will eventually return in the face of all evidence to the contrary, and this belief often prevents them from taking any steps which would signify the end of their marriage or encourage them to think about making a fresh start. Their behaviour may be similar to that of someone who has recently lost a partner through death; that their lost partner may be living down the road and could reappear or be met accidentally at any moment adds an extra twist to their suffering. Grief of this kind is considered in a very helpful book (see Appendix 2) by the psychiatrist, Colin Murray Parkes:

> Grief may not produce physical pain but it is very unpleasant and it usually disturbs function. Thus a newly bereaved person is often treated by society in much the same way as a sick person. Employers expect him to miss work, he stays at home and relatives visit and talk in hushed tones. For a time others take over responsibility for making decisions and acting on his behalf. When the grief is severe the bereaved person may be disabled for weeks, and relatives worry about him; later he may say 'I don't know how I lived through it.'

On the whole, grief resembles a physical injury rather than any other type of illness. The loss may be spoken of as a 'blow'. Parkes argues, however, that although it may be regarded as an illness, grief

> can also bring strength. Just as broken bones may end up stronger than unbroken ones, so the experience of grieving can strengthen and bring maturity to those who have previously been protected from misfortune. The pain of grief is as much a part of life as the joy of love; it is, perhaps, the price we pay for love, the cost of commitment.[11]

People enduring pain of this kind because of a sudden separation need the sort of support we would offer to the bereaved. For a time they may need help with managing day-to-day events and caring for children. At this stage there is little point in trying to persuade them to deal with practical matters or to make decisions about the future. Many divorced people described how, initially, they were reluctant to visit a solicitor or were unwilling to initiate divorce proceedings. Even if they recognized their marriage was over, they did not feel ready to divorce. Sometimes pressing financial and housing problems or decisions about the children may force people into seeking advice and taking action immediately, but if it is at all possible it is better to wait until the person involved is ready to act of their own accord.

It was characteristic of Mr Heathcote, an estate agent in the Sheffield study, that he should throw himself into organizing the aspects of the crisis he felt most familiar with when his wife left him and immediately began to make the arrangements necessary to sell his house. Just after his wife's departure an acquaintance rang him to inquire whether he knew of any semi's for sale in the area:

> I just said, 'Well, would you like to buy mine?' She thought I was joking ... and they came round and left having bought it. Mortgages at the time were impossible to get ...

He rang round his contacts, was eventually offered what was needed, and

> ... the mortgage was done straight away, within the week and everything just went through, just like that, the assistants pulled

their finger out ... and on the fifteenth of May I moved out, which was six weeks after she'd gone.

Others left to cope on their own may busy themselves with less dramatic but equally significant activities, trying to remove all traces of their former partner from their lives; they redecorate their houses, clear out their cupboards, change their cars and take up new projects as they try to cope with the pain and sense of loss the departure of their partner has provoked.

Many people will find it difficult to believe that couples who have fought and destroyed one another to the point of separation would ever actually miss one another, or that they need to grieve for their lost partner as much as those who are unwillingly deserted when a marriage ends, but several people have told me how it was only after they split up that they were able to face a grief and loss which had occurred much *earlier*, when they first felt their marriage was going wrong.

Philip, now in his late forties, is a consultant in a large teaching hospital. He spent the early years of his marriage climbing the medical ladder; like many other doctors, he spent relatively little time with his wife and growing family. He was dimly aware that he and his wife seemed to have less and less in common and that they bickered and argued a lot about domestic details when they were together. Poised and self-sufficient, he withdrew into an all-absorbing professional world, comforting himself that he was able to provide his family with a high standard of living although he rarely had time to enjoy it himself. When he was thirty-two his father died suddenly and painfully. This was the first important personal crisis in his well-ordered life and he was shocked to find that his wife could not help him, and did not even seem to want to. Life continued much as usual for another five years, until, at about the time he took up a more senior post, they began to argue bitterly 'about absolutely everything'. Eventually they decided to split up and she left home. Philip could not, at first, understand why he experienced such strong feelings of loss, for he realized that eventual separation was inevitable and he saw her departure as a relief and an opportunity to make a new beginning 'before it was too late'. He 'fell apart' for several months, scarcely able to cope with the demands of his job and with no energy or inclination for new beginnings. He later recognized that he was mourning for his marriage whose real 'death' had occurred some years earlier. About this time he had several vivid and disturbing dreams which evoked an earlier much happier period when they had been closer and more content. When he remembered times like those he sometimes caught himself wondering why they had split up at all ... until he remembered more recent events.

THE END OF A MARRIAGE

Separation not only provokes a strong sense of loss for your ex-partner but also for the marriage itself, for the identity and position in society which being married provides. This affects some more strongly than others. Couples marrying in their late teens or early twenties who separate after a few years have relatively little to lose when they abandon the married status. They are easily able to rejoin their peers, returning to live with their parents, even if only for a short time, or sharing a flat with other 'single' people. If they have no children they will soon be virtually indistinguishable from the unmarried people they mix with. By contrast, men and women in their forties or fifties who divorce after more than twenty years of marriage lose much more when they stop being married. Women suffer more than men in this respect. Many women still make, or intend to make, marriage their career, so that for those in their forties divorce is a form of redundancy or unemployment with relatively few alternative careers in prospect.

In addition, marriages based on a division of responsibility where one partner works outside the home while the other retains home and children as her domain, encourages a system of interlocking dependencies which leaves both partners ill-equipped for life on their own. In early married life, it may be gratifying to know that your husband cannot manage without your domestic services or that your wife needs you to mend the car – certainly such inter-dependence creates a kind of closeness, adding substance to the lover's claim that (s)he 'cannot live without you'. When this pattern has built up over many years of marriage, newly separated people may find themselves totally unable to cope with those aspects of daily life formerly left to their partners. I recall one man whose wife gave him a small piece of paper when they split up, listing the sizes of his clothes, shoes, etc., as, throughout his married life, he had never bought clothes on his own. Initially, many older women find the world beyond their home completely beyond their grasp. For such men and women their feelings of incompetence are often strengthened by more general beliefs that these new responsibilities are not really men's/women's work. Depressed and lethargic as a result of the crisis of separation, even choosing and cooking an evening meal or remembering to recharge the car battery seem an overwhelming responsibility.

Many of the tiring and mundane routines of daily life are only made more bearable by doing them with, or for, someone else. Newly separated people who do not pass immediately from one couple relationship to another often miss their partner as a day-to-day companion, even if there has been considerable conflict between them. Even when the partner seems to have caused nothing but trouble, forever making difficulties, their departure leaves a gap; if the couple have been sleeping together until the break, the bed now seems much larger and colder at night. Also, even warring partners can provide one another with support in public. It is not unusual for couples who have already decided to split up to avoid telling anyone else, even close family and friends, until the last moment, so they may still appear together at social functions, exercising the long-standing, shared skills necessary to deal with tiresome relatives or troublesome neighbours. In addition, the shell of their marriage may continue to protect them from some of the more unwelcome aspects of being single in a world of couples. When they finally split up, such couples are particularly aware of the everyday losses and deprivations they have sustained.

'WHERE DID WE GO WRONG?'

For a variety of reasons, couples who split up need to be able to offer some sort of explanation for the failure of their marriage. Many newly separated people mention that this unspoken question

41

seems to hang in the air when they declare their marital status in routine encounters with public officials; they feel that they must suggest in some way that they were not responsible for the separation.

The explanations offered to family and friends are usually more complex – indeed, relatives and close friends may actively help the partners towards an understanding of what has happened. Parents, particularly, may claim that they already suspected that something was wrong or confess that, despite apparently successful attempts to get on with their son- or daughter-in-law they had never liked him or her and knew 'it would never last'. Married friends may find the news that a couple in their circle are splitting up very disturbing and look for an explanation which will reassure them that their own marriage is not in danger.

Most importantly, the individuals themselves have a strong need to try and make sense of what has happened to them as they begin to deal with their feelings of loss, guilt and anger. Many of their unspoken questions are concerned with allocation of blame. Although divorce legislation since the Divorce Reform Act 1969 supports the idea of no-fault divorce and is designed to give dead marriages a decent burial, most of us are still convinced that someone must be responsible for the breakdown of a marriage.

Explanations tend to change and evolve with the passage of time. Initially, the actual circumstances of the break-up shape our interpretation of what has happened and who is responsible. Thus, the deserted spouse, victim of his/her partner's infidelities, feels injured and will attract sympathy and support – all the blame seems to lie with the unfaithful partner. Later, as time passes, such one-sided explanations are subject to modification as (s)he begins to consider the past more deeply. For example, folk wisdom suggests that when a married man or woman wanders there is usually something amiss at home. Deserted wives may begin to blame themselves for failing to live up to their image of the ideal wife and home-maker, and deserted husbands may wonder if they have failed to keep their wives because they have not been able to provide as high a standard of living as they would have liked. It is a tragic irony that for both men and women it is sometimes their greatest efforts to ensure the stability of their marriage which eventually cause an unbridgeable rift between them.

Some years afterwards, Mr Heathcote was able to talk with detachment about what went wrong with his marriage. He took on an extra part-time job selling insurance after his second child was born:

> I suppose that was the beginning of the end, as far as my marriage was concerned, because I spent so much time on it ... I started at that point in time to get my priorities in the wrong order ... a part-time job took priority over my wife and kids, not intentionally. I were doing it for their benefit, she wanted to be able to spend money, I'd got to go out and earn it and you can't do that by sitting on your backside.

This was very successful and he eventually decided to leave his secure job as a surveyor with the local authority to start his own business. He needed his wife's signature to raise capital through a second mortgage on their house. He realizes now that this made her very insecure.

> ... all she could see was that I was pulling the carpet away from under her feet and the house would disappear, she'd finish up with nothing, all this sort of thing. She'd got no confidence in her husband that he knew what he was talking about and I suppose it made me even more determined to succeed.

She found a job as a croupier in a night club:

> She started to work in the evening, six nights a week. She had to be there half-past eightish and I was going to see people in the day-time so what used to happen is, I would stay home till lunch, at which time she would get up, then I would leave the house. With a bit of luck I might be home for tea, but it was very rare.
>
> We didn't see each other apart from one night a week and that one night she wanted taking out; she wanted to be wined and dined and then on to a night club ... Many's the time I've fallen asleep in the middle of the main act just absolutely knackered, couldn't cope, you know, ... with working all day up till half-past eight ... That was the beginning of the end then because

she found different outside interests and we gradually grew
further and further apart, er ... [long pause] and I didn't see,
everybody else did but not me. As far as I was concerned I was
flogging my guts out for the benefit of my family ... and it
seemed to be working all right. Of course, after me marriage did
break up everybody used to say, 'ah well, I knew it couldn't last'.
They're always wiser with hindsight, aren't they?

When he first discovered that she was having an affair he cast
himself as the innocent party, shocked and angry at her betrayal
but during the research interviews, as he tried to explain and make
sense of what had happened, he was at pains to show how they had
both grown apart.

The partner who ends the marriage because of an affair with
someone else finds it hard, at least at first, to avoid being cast as
the 'guilty party'. The guilt and uncertainty which plagues them
while they are making up their minds may persist after the actual
decision to separate has been made. Mr Dunwell left his wife very
suddenly to go and live with Jenny, now his second wife:

My feelings of guilt began to build up more and more and it
worried me, what I actually put my first wife through during the
actual events of separation. For some time I felt quite upset
about that ... at times I was quite emotional about it.

He describes how these feelings began to lose their power as the
result of listening to a radio programme:

It was a religious programme on the radio that I happened to
overhear ... I can't remember the exact words ... but it said you
shouldn't keep punishing yourself for things that have happened
in the past, because they're over and done with and you can't
do anything about them.

Guilt of this kind often persists for a long time, sometimes
clouding new relationships and partnerships. When people end
their marriage in order to embark on another relationship immediately, the principal justification is that they 'fell in love', that
almost imperceptibly, an innocent acquaintanceship was trans-
formed into something more significant, something they felt powerless to control. At a later stage it may be necessary to try to explain

why they were so vulnerable at that particular time, in order to demonstrate that things had already begun to go wrong in their marriage. When they look back, many divorced people feel that they were too young when they first married or that the circumstances of their life have changed them beyond reunion or reconciliation with their first partners. Mr Thompson, now a youth worker, first got married when he was in the air force:

> I think our marriage was sort of immature from the start, really ... we were both immature and in the forces you don't tend to mature until you leave. I didn't; I was still immature at twenty-seven when I went to college.

The problems of making sense of the past, trying to come to terms with the failure of a marriage, may also involve a reevaluation of other areas of our lives. The writer A. Alvarez describes his feelings shortly after separation:

> I felt ashamed. Not taken aback, not angry, not socially embarrassed – I left that to my parents, although they never complained – simply ashamed at such undeniable, comprehensive failure. Until then I thought I could do anything if I tried ... And because I had a small gift in one area and competence in several, I assumed everything would be forgiven and forgotten. Now I discovered that my account had been scrupulously kept and I had to pay the whole score: the evasions, the sleights of mind and tricks of style, the white lies, missed appointments, unanswered letters. All of them had been called in by this marriage. Failure in that cancelled out the successes elsewhere and revived failures I thought I had forgotten or hadn't even recognized. Every last one of them.[12]

It is not so surprising that so many people 'fall apart' in one way or another. Overwhelmed by the ever-present problems of everyday life, battered by unanswerable questions about the past and anxiety about the future, they search for answers. 'Can I afford to pay the gas bill?' 'How do you cook scrambled eggs without ruining the saucepan?' 'Why do I feel so tired?' 'Did he ever really love me?' 'Was it moving to Bristol that spoilt everything?' 'Will I be able to hang on to this job?' 'Will things work out for me in future?'

Making sense of the past, through talking and thinking things out, is an important part of the healing process. It provides us with some answers to our own and other people's questions about what went wrong. It is also the first stage in the formulation of a blueprint for the future. Singing about a relationship which seems to be over, Art Garfunkel struggles to face the future:

> Something inside me needs to know I
> can live to love again.
> What is now has always been.
> I need to let you know.

GETTING IT TOGETHER

> ... for a couple of weeks I was feeling very sorry for myself and then I, sort of, grabbed myself by the roots and said to myself, 'Come on, carry on with a new life from now on, this one is over, start anew, it's no good hanging on to what you haven't got.'

In some ways the crisis of a partner's sudden and unexpected desertion has its compensations; the shock may precipitate a sufficiently serious collapse to allow the victim to withdraw into illness for a time. Friends and family rally round, relieving you of everyday responsibilities; they give you 'permission' to mourn, to release your pain in bouts of rage and weeping. They provide a listening ear as you rework the past, seeking explanation and reassurance. When, in due time, you begin to recover sufficiently to heed their advice, to put the past behind you and start again, you have had an opportunity to express some of your feelings – an opportunity all too often denied to separating partners in other circumstances.

Mike, a teacher, told me how he had been having an affair for over a year when his wife found out, seemingly by accident although he had been looking for a way of telling her for some time. They stayed together for another six weeks while he helped her to make the necessary arrangements to take on the tenancy of their flat and to find a childminder so that she could return to work. They organized their finances, worked out how he would see the children regularly and divided their possessions. He took very little away

46

with him because he was going to move in with his girlfriend, Susie, who already had a place of her own. On the night before he left, most of the conflict seemed to be over; they talked into the early hours, sharing some of their memories of the past. Both seemed genuine in their hope that they would each be happy in the future. When he arrived at Susie's place after work that evening she had prepared a celebration meal with a bottle of wine – for her their new life together was beginning. But Mike felt more depressed and alone than he had ever done before. Unprepared to think about starting again just yet, he described himself as alone, set apart in a no man's land between the past and the future.

Starting afresh is frequently symbolized by marked changes in domestic arrangements. Wives left with the matrimonial home must learn to organize it without the help formerly given by their husbands and usually with a great deal less money available. Husbands who leave, unless like Mike they have girlfriends to shelter them, often find themselves returning to parents or starting life in flats and bedsitters with a standard of living they thought they had left behind years ago. In such circumstances it is often brought home to us how much we have come to rely on familiar domestic routines and valued possessions to shape the texture of our daily lives. In this sense, starting again means finding our own solutions to the problems of everyday domestic life and creating our own routines. (Tea or coffee first thing in the morning? Radio Four, Two or Capital? Launderette or washing machine? Surplus money to be spent on books or records or a good night out?)

The first weeks or months may be simply spent in getting by, learning to survive on the money available, finding and organizing new accommodation, forcing yourself to work and collapsing at night in front of the television. A number of people have told me of the powerful hold television had over them during these early months. They became avid followers of all the soap operas, organizing their routine so that they could follow them night by night. Exhausted by the complexities of their own daily lives they preferred, for a time, to experience human relationships at second-hand, safely locked behind the television screen.

Those who, for a variety of reasons, felt very constrained by their marriage, may be ready to start again almost immediately.

47

Sometimes you meet a friend or acquaintance whom you have not seen for a long time:

'My, you're looking well. You look ten years younger. Have you just won the pools?'

'No, actually Jack/Jane and I split up six months ago, and since then I've had a whole new lease of life.'

Mr Heathcote reorganized his domestic life, selling his house and moving in with his mother so that she could look after the children:

> I suddenly woke up one day and I thought to myself, 'Well, you're a bloody fool; you're only young,' and then I met a girl and then I met another and then for a period of about twelve months I went ... I went out ... I had six girlfriends at a time, all of 'em wanted to jump into bed with me, which was incredible really when you think about it ... er, unbelievable in fact ... I was thirty-five, two kids, a dog, er ... Who wants me? I thought I was past it, over the hill. Of course I was completely wrong.

Thus, as he discovered, 'getting over it' and 'starting again' also mean testing your new identity in a variety of relationships. Leaving aside immediate family relationships, which we will be considering in the next chapter, the newly separated also have to renegotiate their contacts with friends and in-laws. When couples who split up want to avoid seeing each other again they often try to divide up their friends as they might their books, records or pictures. Much depends on whose friends they were in the first place and on who is cast as the guilty partner, as well as on the tensions and conflicts inherent in the relationship before the split occurred. If you have always disliked your sister-in-law, one of the smaller compensations of divorce is being absolved from ever having to be nice to her again. Similarly people who have made friends as a couple may discover that one of them had merely been tolerating a particular set of friends for the sake of their partner, so that they do not much mind losing contact. If one of the partners has been more active in making and sustaining their friendships the other will feel very isolated after the separation.

For a time at least, as we have seen, failure in marriage may cast its shadow over every aspect of our lives so that 'starting again' involves a positive assertion that we *can* get our lives together once more; success in a particular aspect of life often lifts our spirits and increases our confidence generally. For example, an outwardly confident professional woman in her mid-thirties described how she tried to pull herself together after splitting up from the man with whom she had lived for several years. For the first time, she began to get fit and participate in sports:

> I thought at first that I would never really be able to play well. It seemed as if all the significant people in my entire life had been telling me how clumsy and uncoordinated I was. One day I played with an attractive man whose skill and sureness were beautiful to behold. Afterwards I said how much I enjoyed playing, but that I would never really be any good because I was so clumsy. He turned and looked at me with complete amazement, 'But you're not' – I never looked back from that moment.

A year later she walks tall; the physical poise and confidence that had eluded her all her life now contribute greatly to her strength of character and enjoyment of life.

Separation often forces people to develop skills which had formerly been their partner's responsibility. As well as undermining traditional, strait-jacketed views about what men and women can or cannot do, acquiring unfamiliar skills often enables adults to explore interests and aspects of their character which may have been stifled in their marriage. I am always surprised and slightly alarmed when, in casual conversation, married people pronounce so emphatically on their partner's interests and skills or lack of them; so often the implicit message behind 'Ian *never* cooks' or 'Katie isn't ambitious' really seems to be 'I wouldn't want Ian to get interested in cooking,' or 'I would be afraid if Katie were to get too ambitious.' Freed from such constraints and forced by circumstances into learning new skills, men and women often discover that they really enjoy choosing interior decorations, cooking or gardening after all, or, at least, that they can make a passable job of decorating, household budgeting or mending punctures when necessary.

The sense of failure which pervades the aftermath of a broken marriage frequently erodes confidence about making and sustaining relationships. Sometimes in the final stages of an unhappy marriage both partners begin to speak frankly, recalling old wounds and misunderstandings and rehearsing the things they now say they have never liked about their partner. History is rewritten in a way which suggests they have been desperately unhappy for a long time or even from the very beginning. Both become increasingly confused about how they should interpret past events or evaluate their own behaviour. In such circumstances they will be very scared of making new commitments, and, at this stage at least, are unlikely to want to marry again. Having gained their freedom initially they look for sources of enjoyment far removed from the cosy domesticity of day-to-day married life.

It is very common for newly separated or divorced women and men to describe having a series of short, relatively uncommitted affairs with sexual pleasure and exploration as their main aim. After her first marriage ended, Mrs Hutchinson lived with a younger man for a short time:

> Then I turfed him out and went through a pretty black depression. I were on my own and I didn't really care about anybody else and what they thought of me or anything and I started to, sort of, bed hop then. There were two or three and they were really lads so they were quite a lot younger than me. I don't know, they fulfilled a need but they weren't much good, if you know what I mean. It just left me feeling disgusted with myself and I packed it all in as a bad job and stayed at home for a while ... became a recluse and I thought, 'Oh, from one extreme to the other.'

Attitudes to sex and moral standpoints are acquired from many sources. Many of our basic responses are learnt in childhood and later modified through our own direct experiences. Our understanding of male and female sexuality, our own sexual preferences, as well as our image of our own sexual attractiveness, even, perhaps, how 'good' we are at sex, all develop gradually, modified by different kinds of experiences and relationships. Sexual confidence is not usually at its greatest at the end of marriage. Where longstanding sexual difficulties have gradually driven people further and further apart, they may dimly believe that there might be more to sexual relationships than they have experienced so far, but they are unlikely to be brimming with confidence. One man in the Sheffield study struggled to describe the sexual side of his first marriage:

> She were never affectionate, sexual-wise she's very, what shall I say, straight ... she'd been brought up in a funny way ... she never let herself go. We didn't have a great whizz in bed ... or anything like that. A poor sort of marriage as far as sex were concerned.

Couples who enjoy a good sexual relationship at first find that sexual difficulties arise when other aspects of their relationship begin to deteriorate. Sex becomes a battlefield from which it is easier to withdraw rather than risk rejection or humiliation. Mr Turner described how his former wife had ended his confidence through her constant complaints about his failure to satisfy her:

> I'd lost interest, lack of confidence shall I say, rather than losing interest. It was the confidence side of it that was the problem. When all the knives are thrown, they're usually thrown at you in that respect by your former partner ... it scarred me for a long, long time.

Many people find that relationships with few strings attached provide an opportunity to reaffirm, or perhaps to discover for the first time, confidence in their own sexuality and to blot out negative images of the unsatisfactory or unresponsive lover pressed upon them by former partners.

HOW LONG WILL I FEEL LIKE THIS?

In the first agony of loss, whenever it occurs – and, as we have already seen, it does not always coincide with separation or the formal end of a marriage – we wonder how long will it go on and doubt that we will be able to bear it. Everyone asks at some stage, 'How long will I go on feeling like this?' 'Will it ever get any better?' but there are no easy answers to such questions. Our circumstances and resources differ, along with our capacity to transcend suffering and put the past behind us.

Those who try to comfort friends or relatives going through a marital crisis may feel powerless to help; reassurances that grief will pass, that the sufferer will eventually feel better, seem useless. For a time (s)he can only hang on from moment to moment.

There are, perhaps, some guidelines – where the marriage ends suddenly, acute incapacitating shock usually diminishes within months. (I am sure that that sounds all too callous to anyone going through such pain.) Anyone who still feels completely unable to cope, marooned in their grief after three or four months certainly needs help. Anyone who still has serious problems sleeping or eating, or who is still overcome by frequent bouts of uncontrollable weeping several months later should visit their doctor with as clear an account of how they feel as possible.

Where the separation has been more gradual, reaction may come later. Debilitating periods of gloom and depression, loss of energy and confidence, waking unusually early and starting the day badly are all signs of reaction to personal stress which need attention if they persist. Doctors who have studied the effects of family bereavements on surviving relatives consider that most people will have recovered as much as they ever will within nine to eighteen months. It would be trite and unfeeling to suggest that complete recovery is even possible, but by the end of this time most people are ready to put the past behind them, taking up the threads of an altered life which brings compensations as well as occasional painful reminders of the past.

During this period of recovery, various family anniversaries will pass and it is comforting to realize that you have put behind you the first Christmas, the first summer holiday, the children's birthdays, the reminders prompted by the changing seasons. As time goes on you begin to lay new foundations – daily rituals and routines, special occasions and bits of family history – which mark the beginnings of life after separation. Although the actual anniversary of the day you split up may bring back painful reminders, it also marks the end of this most difficult year.

GETTING HELP

By the time we reach adult life, most of us have developed our own
strategies for dealing with our reactions to stress and personal
setbacks. We may already know who we can safely rely on for
practical help and support; who will take the children off our hands
for a bit or listen to us as we work through financial problems
and our plans for the future. Our first response to crisis is often
extreme: either we bottle everything up, unable to share our pain
and confusion with even our closest friends, or we find ourselves
talking about our problems almost continuously. A friend described how, after her teenage son's death in a motor-cycle accident, she had her milkman holed up in the porch for three-quarters
of an hour while she obsessively rehearsed all the details of the
accident. It is important for those involved in separation to find
someone to whom they can talk freely. It is easier to make sense
of what has happened when we can tell our story freely, recognizing
the strong feelings which were aroused by the events described. It
is usually only when we have come to terms with the pain and
reached a satisfactory explanation of what has happened that we
can relinquish the past and begin to build afresh.

This kind of sharing also helps us to prepare for the more formal
discussion of our feelings, circumstances and problems which is
necessary when we seek professional help and advice of various
kinds. If we have worked out with a friend what we need to ask
when we visit a solicitor or doctor, we are more likely to find the
visit helpful. Unfortunately, doctors do not always have the
necessary time, skills or experience to deal with the more general
problems involved and the help provided by solicitors varies
enormously; many such encounters fail because the client is expecting too much and is disappointed when their difficulties are not
immediately understood or appreciated. If the person who is seeking help can outline their particular needs and problems clearly,
and describe the kind of support they hope for, advisers can assess
realistically the extent to which they will be able to help. Solicitors,
for example, may not want to listen to a full-blown account of what
went wrong while they are trying to gather information on grounds
for the divorce petition. Similarly GPs will not necessarily ask

53

about the underlying reasons for insomnia, back pain, indigestion or anxiety about a child's behaviour if the patient does not offer some hint or direct information. Incidentally, if you want to talk to your GP at length it is sensible to ask for a longer appointment beforehand rather than joining an evening surgery.

CHAPTER 3

Parents but no Longer Partners

Parents who split up have to face up to an additional loss not experienced by childless couples; whether they have custody of their children or not, family life as they formerly experienced it is now over for them. Even when their life together has been ridden by conflict and unhappiness in its latter stages, they often feel that once they have split up they are no longer a 'proper' family.

In everyday terms, it is children who make a family. Newly married couples are asked when they are going to 'start a family'; we refer to men with children – but significantly not women – as 'family men'. By the same token a 'proper' family has two parents; the label 'one-parent family' makes this very clear. When parents split up, each member of the family group has to come to terms with the changes this separation brings for them.

The vast majority of divorced parents are legally, as in daily life, classified either as 'custodial' or 'non-custodial' parents according to whether their children are living with them under their care or not. Some of the sections later in this chapter deal with the particular problems of each of these groups, but please do not skip the sections which do not appear to apply to you – many of the greatest problems of divorced parents arise, in part at least, as a result of their inability to understand their ex-partner's position and feelings about the children for whom they still strive to *share* responsibility.

WHAT ARE WE DOING TO THE CHILDREN?

No one can give a definitive answer to this question, although, as you would expect, it is one which is asked very frequently. It is almost impossible to answer for two main reasons. Firstly, there is still very little satisfactory research on how parental divorce affects children. Despite, or perhaps because of, the rising divorce rate, there seems to be a conspiracy of silence surrounding its human and social consequences and social scientists have not generally been encouraged to carry out work in this area. Secondly, there are many formidable problems in designing such research, as so many issues and variables are involved. While more reliable data would be of immense value to policy-makers and practitioners working in this area, it will always be impossible to use such findings to predict what will happen in any particular case.

In recent years, there has been a good deal of public discussion of the findings of an American study, *Surviving the Breakup* by Wallerstein and Kelly (see Appendix 2). Although it offers us a vivid picture of the feelings of a particular group of children about their parents' divorce, there are important differences between patterns of family life in our own society and those in one of the most affluent areas of the United States.

Questions about how divorce affects children are generally of two kinds. Firstly, how do people whose parents divorced while they were still children differ from those who come from 'unbroken' homes? Secondly, what are the more immediate effects of parental conflict, the uncertainty, upheaval and changes brought about by their separation and the potential deprivations suffered by one-parent families? For our purpose, the second is more important because an understanding of how children may be feeling at the time their parents separate helps us to be more alert to their fears and anxieties and, on occasion, may even enable us to plan and manage some aspects of this separation in a way which avoids unnecessary distress.

In the longer term most parents, whatever their circumstances, go through periods when they worry a good deal about their children's behaviour and achievements, and how they will eventually turn out. Many of the divorced parents in the Sheffield study blamed themselves whenever they experienced difficulties with their children, so that the problems and setbacks experienced by *all* parents – poor school reports, minor delinquencies and bad behaviour – were seen as a direct result of the upheavals of the past.

Even parents who had no particular worries about their children at the time they were interviewed still seemed very anxious about the future, fearing that the suffering their children had experienced in the past would have permanent consequences. In such circumstances a dry recital of research findings which suggest that there is little proven evidence of any long-term effects amongst children of divorced parents is of little consolation. It seems much more important that individual parents should be encouraged to think about their particular situation and develop a greater understanding of their own resources and potential to help their children through the inevitable period of distress and the changes in circumstances caused by the separation.

I have known a number of parents who had bitterly regretted the failure of their marriage and felt very guilty about it, but who were nevertheless able to take comfort that, in their children's interests, they did their best to make their divorce work. Although it was difficult and painful they learnt how to be parents but not partners.

DECIDING ABOUT CUSTODY

The first problem which follows from a couple's decision to live apart is to decide who the children will live with – in formal legal terms, who will have custody. The majority of divorced couples do not discuss this issue at all as it is taken for granted that the children's mother will look after them. For most couples this is a continuation of the way they shared their family and domestic responsibilities within their marriage, and conforms to the conventional ideas of how things 'ought' to be. Despite considerable changes in society's beliefs about the role of women, there is a good deal of research which suggests that mothers are still regarded as being primarily responsible for how children develop as well as for daily child care.[13] Most fathers still spend relatively little time with their children, especially when the children are very young.[14] In addition those fathers who do bring up children on their own are widely regarded as much less capable than single mothers.[15] Thus parents who look to conventional views and practices to decide who should care for the children find that it is usually taken for granted that the mother should have custody, especially when the children are young. Economic and material considerations reinforce this view, as the father usually earns more.

Fathers are awarded custody of their children in about 10 to 15 per cent of cases. This happens most often when the mother leaves home, so that their father has already looked after the children for some time when the arrangement is crystallized in the formal award of custody. Only a very small number of divorcing parents contest the custody of their children, and in such cases the legal decision most frequently confirms the arrangements existing at the time of the hearing.[16] We do not know very much about how most divorcing parents arrive at their decision, but there is a good deal of evidence from solicitors and social workers and others that conflict, disappointment and a sense of failure persist long after the formal divorce and custody proceedings are over, and that divorced partners find it difficult to put the past behind them and cooperate as parents.

If it is at all possible separating parents do need to discuss together the implications of their decision on custody, and it may be helpful for them to consider *all* the alternatives rather than simply assuming that the children should be with their mother. If a father's claim as a potential sole parent is genuinely considered at this time, then both parents will place a high priority on setting up arrangements which encourage maximum contact between the children and their non-custodial parent. It also makes it easier for them to reassess, and if necessary alter, their arrangements in the future if changes in their circumstances or the children's needs suggest this. In addition, if they have shared in this decision it will be easier for them to convey to their children that, whatever their differences, they are prepared to stand by a decision which has been made in the children's interests. This is particularly important when, as often happens, children begin to play one parent off against another.

In this country, joint custody orders are still very unusual. When they are made, one parent has 'care and control' of their children and will be responsible for looking after them on a day-to-day basis but both parents take equal responsibility for the long-term welfare of their children, sharing decisions about, for example, schooling, religious upbringing and so on. This arrangement reflects what some divorced parents regard as ideal and try hard to achieve, so that for such parents the formal legal recognition of their intentions in a joint custody order may help them to crystallize the nature of their continuing commitments as parents.

There is evidence that joint custody orders are sometimes imposed upon couples who have not been able to reach agreement about custody on their own. Learning to cooperate as divorced parents involves recognizing the difficulties and making real compromises, not just papering over the cracks. If you are still doubtful about your own, or your partner's, capacity to do this, joint custody is not for you at this stage, although there is nothing to prevent you from returning to court to change the order later.

Perhaps the preceding pages seem so idealistic, so far from reality, that you are tempted to drop this book into the nearest wastepaper basket. Your husband or wife may have disappeared suddenly and without trace, and your children have no contact with him or her. Or you may be locked in lengthy legal disputes over custody, which have passed beyond your control and are now managed by solicitors, court officials or social workers. Or again, you may be finding it impossible to sit down and talk calmly with your ex-partner about the most pressing problems – about money, housing and the children, the very issues which have been most likely to provoke conflict throughout your married life. In some areas, there is now a conciliation service available to separating couples (see Appendix 1). Parents are given the opportunity of discussing the outstanding problems about their children with a neutral third party who understands both the legal background and the kinds of feelings and anxieties which are common at this time. Marriage Guidance counsellors are also prepared to help couples to talk about their children together, even if they have already decided to split up (see Appendix 1). Details of a variety of divorce experience courses are also included in Appendix 1. Other couples may prefer to find a trusted friend to whom they can both talk about their children's future.

Sometimes parents who reach agreement about custody and access fairly easily at the time they actually separate find that difficulties arise months or even years later. In this case they too may need someone who can act as an impartial third party while they try to work out their problems together, before resorting to formal legal proceedings over access or custody arrangements.

I am often asked how much of a say the children themselves should have when decisions about custody are being made. This question mirrors the tension, felt by everyone who cares for children in one capacity or another, between the need to be a 'protector' and a 'liberator' – the need to cherish the weak and dependent and, at the same time, encourage growth, autonomy and independence in children. It is often very difficult to get just the right balance. However, in this instance, while children need to be given appropriate opportunities to make decisions and take responsibility for many aspects of their own lives, we cannot expect them to foresee the consequences of decisions which even the adults responsible for them shrink from making. Asking them for their views, helping them to talk about what they like and dislike about being with each parent and about the pain and loss they feel when they say goodbye at the end of a visit is a very different matter from pressing the burden of decision-making upon them. This became very plain to me when I was asked to talk to a friend's thirteen-year-old daughter, Louise, about her parents' separation some six months earlier. Both now had new partners and she had spent several months with each of them. Each home had its advantages and, although they both wanted her to live with them, they also seemed genuinely prepared to put her needs first. They had tried to talk to her about it but found her unusually incommunicative. She came to my office as it was near her school and as I made her a cup of coffee she asked me very directly why her father had asked her to come and talk to me. Still busy with the coffee, I said I thought her parents each wanted her to live where she would be happiest and that her parents both wanted to know more about how she felt before they decided what was best for her. 'I thought they wanted me to decide,' she burst out angrily. I sat down slowly, carefully stirring my coffee. 'No, I don't think so, it's not really your decision. Tom and Anna are still your parents even though they don't live together . . . but they do want to know what you feel before they make up their minds . . . There are a lot of important things involved, schools, Tom's step-children, Anna's new baby ...' She relaxed, slumping back in my easy chair and we talked about the kind of life she had with each of her parents. It soon became clear that what she most wanted was to have more say in the organization and timing of visits to both her parents, as she did not want to be cut off from her friends. She was very clear that she did not want the responsibility of deciding where she would live and go to school, as she felt she would be bound to hurt and disappoint one or other of them. Her parents had made the decisions which led to their eventual separation and divorce; their continuing responsibility for Louise included being prepared to make decisions about her future, and to live with, and work through, the consequences of these decisions.

SEPARATION AND AFTER FROM A CHILD'S POINT OF VIEW

Just as some adults will find it hard to say precisely when and how their marriage ended, it is also difficult for the children involved. Some children gradually become aware that their father is spending more and more time 'away on business', 'working late', 'playing golf' or 'down at the pub', and that even when they are together their parents do not seem to have much to say to one another. Others, reluctant witnesses of sarcasm, bickering, arguments and even physical violence, are left in no doubt about their parents' feelings for one another. Even the most sudden and apparently unexpected separations, when one partner leaves with little or no warning, are often preceded by changes in atmosphere which do not usually pass unnoticed. As a result, they are often far more prepared than might be expected when their parents begin to try to explain what is happening. Talking openly is often a great relief, as they are given information which will help them to make sense of things they had not been able to understand before. It is also an opportunity to air their anxieties about changes already taking place and some of their fears about the future.

Whatever age we are, many of us find change disturbing and unsettling and we respond by clinging even more closely to familiar routines and landmarks. Children are often more obvious about this and their first questions after being told that their parents are splitting up may seem startlingly callous or materialistic: 'If we move house, will there be room for my rabbit?', 'Will I still be getting a new bicycle for Christmas?'

When they find explanations and long-term consequences hard to absorb they try to work out how the new situation will affect the framework of their own lives, their friendships, their daily routine and the relationships which give them security. Similarly, concern about how this will affect each of their parents is likely to be demonstrated in very practical terms. Questions like 'Who will iron daddy's shirts if he lives on his own?' and 'Won't Mum be cold in bed all on her own?' mirror preoccupations less easily put into words.

Once we understand a child's overwhelming need for the security of familiar routines and continuity in daily life, we can take this into account as we talk to them and make plans. Certain changes are unavoidable and these should be faced quite openly. It is tempting to soothe an anxious, overwrought child with promises that nothing will change, but in the long run nobody benefits when promises are made to children which it will be impossible to keep. For example, you may realize that moving house is inevitable and your children need to be prepared for this but you should try to talk to them about how it affects each of them in practical terms rather than wasting your breath on complicated financial explanations or blaming it on 'Daddy's new girlfriend'. Moving house may involve a change of schools; friends and relatives may not be so easily accessible and there may be a reduction in play facilities at home, if, for example, you no longer have a garden or room for a full size table-tennis table. It is not necessary to talk about everything at once but be prepared to go at their pace, facing up to all that they believe these changes are going to mean to them. Recognizing some changes are unavoidable, many parents try to preserve as much continuity as they can in other areas of their children's lives. Sometimes this entails the expenditure of precious and limited energy in small ways by keeping up family mealtime and bedtime rituals, or may involve more careful planning. A newly separated woman, normally extremely independent and self-reliant, told me how she eventually decided to take up a new friend's offer of help. She and the children had moved to a different area and were settling down well but her eight-year-old daughter missed the ballet class she used to go to on the other side of the city. Her friend drove the child to her ballet class every week, while she stayed at home and cooked an evening meal for both families.

As we have already seen in the previous chapter, most adults find that the emotional stress of separation leads to physical or mental illness of one sort or another at some stage between the onset of the first doubts and the time when they are ready to 'start again'. Parents suddenly left in sole charge of their children when their partner leaves unexpectedly sometimes collapse completely for a short time. They are fortunate if they have friends, neighbours or a relative who can come in and look after them and the children, but it is not unusual for children to be sent to stay with relatives for a while, or even to be placed in temporary care of the local authority while the parent recovers. Being apart from their remaining parent at this time is bound to make children feel much worse. They often feel that they are in some way responsible for their parent's departure and become very anxious that their other parent might disappear as well; sending them away thus adds immeasurably to their distress. If this is the only solution, it is important to explain exactly what is happening and to reassure them that the arrangement is only temporary.

Anxiety about being separated from their remaining parent is at the root of much of the worrying behaviour of children during this difficult time. They often seem to go back to an earlier stage when they were cared for more closely by their parents. They may, for example, start to wet the bed again after many years of being dry. They may be very unhappy about being parted from their mother, refusing to stay at playgroup or at school, or they may become unusually awkward or demanding. One of the mothers featured in the radio programmes described the difficulties she had in getting her son to go to school:

He tried not to go to school. Every morning we had a fight. He didn't want to wear certain clothes. We had to struggle to get him into a car. He used to take his jumpers and things off in the car. Eventually the headmistress suggested not sending him until he really wanted to go to school, and apparently it was because he didn't want to leave home. He was feeling pretty insecure.

Children can also express their anxiety by being unusually, even unnaturally, well-behaved and cooperative, believing that their virtue and self-discipline will ward off their worst fears. Such anxieties about separation often persist into adult life. For me the only obvious legacy of my mother's death when I was eight is a crippling sense of panic whenever someone I care about does not telephone or arrive if I am definitely expecting them. As the hours slip by, I keep myself going by obsessively acting normally, convinced that steady application to my evening's work, or a pile of ironing or – most impossible of all – going to sleep as usual will restore them safe and sound! My friends have learnt to pander to my anxieties with telephone calls, however inconvenient, if they are delayed; in the same way, children need to be reassured and offered daily confirmation that, although their remaining parent has to leave them from time to time they will always return when expected. Parents who have difficulty in persuading their children to go off with their non-custodial parent on an access visit sometimes find that such anxieties are at the root of their children's reluctance to leave their usual, familiar surroundings. When the custodial parent is still angry with and distrustful of their former partner, it is easy to seize on any excuse to put off the meeting, but it is worth trying to find some compromise. Perhaps the non-custodial partner could stay at home with the child while the other parent goes out, or could arrange to meet them at a friend's or grandparent's until the child feels more confident about leaving home?

In the first months following the end of a marriage, both partners feel bruised, angry and resentful. As they separate emotionally, reminding one another in many trivial but painful ways that they are no longer a couple, their children are both the reason for, and often the only means of, continuing communication. It is not surprising that discussions about any and every aspect of the children's welfare can become a battlefield. In the first months of

coping on their own many parents find that all their plans and
energies are focused on their children; their own needs and anxieties
are submerged or deflected on to their children. Overwhelmed by
the uncertainties and potential dangers which seem to surround
them on all sides, they find that they are unusually anxious about
their children. They begin to make new and more restrictive rules
about being away from home, playing with 'undesirable' friends or
engaging in potentially hazardous hobbies or pursuits. When their
children complain or challenge them, their justification is that they
now have to carry the burden of disciplining and protecting their
children from harm entirely on their own. For a time at least many
of their own more diffuse anxieties about learning to cope alone are
focused specifically on their children.

Children may also be used as a means of communicating with an
ex-partner who seems to be slipping beyond reach. Separated
parents frequently use children as spies, go-betweens and message-
carriers, but in desperation some lone parents may be driven to
gaining their ex-partner's attention by the only method now available, making them feel anxious about their children. Let us consider
the same imaginary but familiar incident from both sides. She is
alone at the weekend; her teenage son and daughter are out with
friends. What are they doing? What kind of trouble might they get
into? While she is worrying about them, the younger son is brought
back, long after the time he was expected, by a neighbour who has
given him a lift from the bus terminus. This gives her the excuse she
has been waiting for. She telephones her ex-husband and pours out
an exaggerated account of their son's misdeeds . . . Her ex-husband
has just settled down to watch the late-night film on TV with his
girlfriend when the telephone rings. He has become used to such
calls and listens to her outpourings with half an eye on the film. As
his girlfriend's sympathetic gestures and signs become increasingly
impatient, he becomes angry and uncomfortable. It is hard to make
much sense of what his wife is saying and when she suggests that
their son has just come home smelling of cannabis he decides to go
over straight away. As he leaves his flat, his girlfriend is clattering
the washing-up angrily in the kitchen . . .

In the radio programmes we included a very vivid example of the
way children may be used as a means of communicating parents'

fears. Shortly after the birth of their son, John, Mel finally left home to go and live with Marge, whom he later married. Sue, his wife, had known about this affair throughout her pregnancy and was now desperate to get him to return permanently. On the night Mel left, Sue gave John, only nine weeks old, some of her sedatives.

> I gave John some of the phenobarbitones I was taking at the time ... Coldly and calmly I crushed the tablets and put them in his bottle but I wasn't aware that this was going to hurt John. Obviously, deep down within me all I wanted was to have Mel back. I didn't realize the seriousness of how it almost killed John. I think I was thinking that if things weren't quite all right and the baby wasn't well, he wouldn't go.

She later took John to hospital and he suffered no permanent harm but as a result she lost custody of both her children. After a five-year break she now sees them regularly.

Such desperate measures are unusual; they were the culmination of a prolonged period of uncertainty and ill-health, but many single parents will recognize the stress of knowing that their ex-partner can now only be reached through fuelling anxieties about the children.

WHY IS IT SO DIFFICULT TO BE A SINGLE PARENT?

Once they get over the initial shock, organize themselves and adapt to their changed standard of living, some single parents eventually begin to wonder what all the fuss is about. A divorced woman, Carol, described her marriage to a long-distance lorry driver:

> I've been a single parent in all but name since my first baby were born ... he sees more of his children now we've got definite visiting arrangements, which his new wife sees he sticks to, than he ever did when he lived here. My biggest problem now is that they've written us down as a one-parent family up at the school and whenever there's any trouble, our Chris says he gets singled out because he comes from a broken home.

Myths about broken homes abound in many school staffrooms and, I am ashamed to say, sometimes originate from the training courses followed by student teachers, social workers and health workers. Sometimes such labels can be consciously turned to advantage, as one of the teenagers in our radio programmes found. He had been arrested for burglary a year before and he was asked whether he thought his behaviour had been affected by his parents' divorce:

> No, I don't think it had anything to do with it whatsoever ... because the actual divorce was about eight years ago and I hadn't been in any trouble all through that, till I was sixteen and that was the last time, so I can't see any relevance to it at all ... At the time it just seemed exciting, I didn't think I'd get caught and at the time it was, well it seemed, good fun. Of course afterwards you're full of regret and everything, and it hasn't happened since.

When his case came to court he was surprised to find that

> they did make a lot of emphasis on the fact that I came from a one-parent family and I was supposed to have had an unhappy childhood. I was quite stunned in court actually when they read out all the things that was supposed to have happened to me and what I'd been through. Quite frankly I never knew the half of it ... but I did actually get away very lightly, so I think that's the reason why it all came out.

In this instance, David's 'label' was made to work for him but most parents and children find the stigma of belonging to a one-parent family very distressing. If teachers, medical people or social workers ever try to explain your problems away as the natural, even inevitable consequence of a broken home it is worth trying to challenge their assumptions by asking further questions. There are a number of very helpful books which deal fully with every aspect of single parenthood (see Appendix 2). In addition, *Gingerbread Magazine* and *One Parent Times*, the journal of the National Council for One Parent Families, often include articles which will help you to develop sufficient confidence to put your own informed point of view when you feel your child is being unfairly labelled. Parents in a similar situation can also give you much-needed support.

MONEY PROBLEMS

Nevertheless, most myths do have some basis in reality. What then, are adults and children in a one-parent family most likely to lack? The first and most significant answer is money – a large proportion of one-parent households live at, or below, the poverty line. A second and related deprivation is that they frequently have less time and energy available for the ordinary activities of family and domestic life than other families. If the husband's task is to earn money outside the home and his wife takes responsibility for most of the work within the home, the whole household suffers if either of them disappears. As fathers left on their own quickly discover, keeping the family together depends as much on the unpaid, and sometimes unrecognized, labour of child care and domestic work as on the wage packet. When either member of the team withdraws, the household's standard of living is bound to deteriorate. With the best will in the world, departing fathers cannot make as great a contribution to the support of their families as they did when they lived together, especially if they intend to marry again and want to start a new family. Even when maintenance is paid regularly and in full, all the members of divorced families will be worse off financially than they were before they split up. Many one-parent families in Britain face serious poverty. One study carried out for the Finer Report, suggested that between 1969 and 1971 almost half of one-parent families were living below or near the official poverty line, the level at which Supplementary Benefit is set.

HOW DOES POVERTY AFFECT CHILDREN?

The relative decline in their standard of living experienced by divorced families may in reality be more of a problem to parents than to their children. We live in a society in which our personal and public success is measured, in part at least, by the successful pursuit of a steadily rising standard of living to be enjoyed within the home and shared amongst members of our immediate family. The material and interpersonal goals of marriage and family life are closely intertwined – persuasive advertising copy almost convinces us that in order to be a good husband/father a man only has to bring home a large and secure income for the 'ideal' wife/mother to invest and consume in a way which enhances the appearance and well-being of each member of the family.

Our children are not immune from such pressures – on occasion, they can easily hurt us by their acute observations of how the family's lower standard of living might affect them – but they are unlikely to worry much about 'coming down in the world' if no real hardship is involved. If your children irritate you because of their constant grumbles about minor deprivations, it may be that they are copying *you*, and reflecting *your* preoccupations rather than their own. In any case, most parents, whatever their financial circumstances, are sometimes irritated by the way their children compare their own pocket money and possessions with those of their friends.

Brian Jackson describes vividly what poverty means for many one-parent families:

> ... an episodic life in which there is never any guarantee that it will get better. It means poor housing, sharing bedrooms, basic food, worries over food and other bills, no holidays. In one sample 75 per cent of children under fourteen never had a birthday party.[17]

Barbara was divorced eight years ago. Her husband has never paid maintenance regularly. She described the constant hassle of

> court, phoning solicitors ... because of not being paid my maintenance and having to rely on social services to check [it].

As a result, there have been occasions when

> I've had men standing on the doorstep ready to cut off the electricity. I've often told the children to say I'm not in when I am, you know, this happens regularly with the milkman and things. I really hit a problem when I had my mother in hospital very ill. I couldn't afford the fare, you know, to go and see her and pay for general housekeeping, so we lived on rice for a fortnight nearly. Things like sheets that need replacing and cups, you know, silly things like that, you just can't go straight out and buy them ...

As Barbara and countless others have found there is very little

69

that you as an individual can do to fight an economic and political system which treats one-parent families so shamefully. Perhaps the most practical thing you can do once you have picked up the pieces is to join with other people in similar circumstances to campaign about family poverty through groups like the National Council for One Parent Families or the Child Poverty Action Group. Much more public attention needs to be drawn to the fact that, although we pay lip-service to the importance of the family and the needs of children, our tax system actually penalizes families;[18] welfare benefits are set at a level so low that most households with children who rely entirely on Supplementary Benefit have great difficulty in making ends meet even over a relatively short period.

Within these constraints single parents need to make sure that they are claiming all they are entitled to, from whatever source. Even the most well-organized and highly educated divorced parents find it very difficult to negotiate the jungles of Supplementary Benefit on the one hand and tax and maintenance rules after separation on the other. In most cases, those who have been in similar circumstances themselves are the most reliable guides. This is another good reason for making an effort to contact a local one-parent family group such as Gingerbread.

Local Citizens' Advice Bureaux, Welfare Rights and Law Centres will help you to sort out what you are entitled to and show you how to claim. They will also recommend other specialist advisers if needed. Local branches of the Claimants' Union also have a good deal of up-to-date information and case material on all aspects of Supplementary Benefit.

The rules surrounding maintenance and taxation after separation have become very complex in recent years and it may be necessary to find a solicitor or accountant who specializes in this field. Try to get a personal recommendation from someone who has had their own finances successfully sorted out after separation; the solicitor who did the conveyancing of your house eight years ago and that 'nice accountant I met at the pub' will not necessarily be experts in the law and finance of divorce.

In the first months after separation there is so much to cope with that it is easy to put off making the necessary financial arrangements. Some are reluctant to take a further unwelcome step towards recognizing that their marriage is over; others hesitate because they know it will inevitably lead to further embittered arguments. As a result, however, people find themselves caught up in unnecessary hardship and uncertainty. For example, when Barbara's ex-husband first left home he paid her no maintenance and, without telling her, stopped paying the rent on their house. Eventually they reached the stage when

> ... bailiffs came in and marked off the furniture, which was awful, and we were under threat of being evicted ... The probation officer said we had to go to court and I had to apply for maintenance because I wasn't receiving any and we were really having a very rough time.

Despite finding the court appearance 'very harrowing', she was awarded maintenance and took over the tenancy of the house, and was then able to make a new beginning.

'ONE OF MY PARENTS IS MISSING'

The very name 'one-parent family' suggests that a household group with only one parent is less than complete. It is worth pointing out that there are many children growing up in one-parent households who have more sustained and caring contact with *both* parents than children in many so-called normal families. Many fathers have to be away from home for prolonged periods for work reasons: members of the armed forces, off-shore oil workers, international businessmen and long-distance lorry drivers for example. Others are forced into patterns of shift-working which mean that they are rarely at home when their children are about. One study of European businessmen shows very clearly that many fathers find that the pressure to stay late at work and to bring piles of papers home at the weekend is often at its greatest at the very stage in a man's career when his children are growing and changing most rapidly. Driven by the satisfaction of his own achievements and his desire to do his best for his wife and family, it is easy for men with interesting and demanding jobs to lose contact with the day-to-day lives of their children. They fulfil only the more formal aspects of a father's role, attending school events, taking the important decisions about O-levels or future careers and so on. Wives who feel they are left too much on their own with their children sometimes try, perhaps unconsciously, to exclude their husbands from *any* involvement in home and family, which has become their domain. Although usually from affluent and privileged homes, these children also should be considered as belonging to a 'one-parent family' in some respects.

One of the greatest advantages of having two parents is that, potentially at least, children have access to more adult interest, attention, energy and loving. When one parent begins to flag or seems unreasonable, there is someone else to turn to. Some parents do not make a clear distinction between the responsibilities and activities of 'father' and 'mother'; they substitute for one another so easily that either would be equally happy to be left in sole charge of the household. Other parents share their responsibilities differently so that while the mothers take primary responsibility for looking after the children, the back-up and support given by their husbands would be greatly missed if it were withdrawn. Even being able to share the exhaustion helps – people who have not had children themselves or whose child-rearing days are long since past rarely appreciate the variety of demands made on parents as their children pass by degrees from demanding babies to rebellious teenagers. Any parent who is bringing up children on their own, for whatever reason, is likely to feel deprived if they feel there is no one with whom they can share both the joys and responsibilities of child care.

Lacking adult company and support, single parents sometimes find themselves trying to make their older children into adult companions. In such circumstances, it is possible that an unwelcome burden is being placed on the children by expecting them to share their parent's preoccupations, especially if they hear embittered damaging revelations about the departed parent. Children who have been encouraged to take a great deal of responsibility at home and who are pushed into a kind of adulthood by staying up late to 'keep mummy company' and sharing in family secrets will find it particularly hard to readjust if their mother remarries and they are then firmly reallocated to the children's generation once again.

Parents who bring up children on their own are often particularly anxious about how their children will develop without the 'missing' adult figure of the opposite gender. Their worries are of two kinds. Single fathers may feel powerless to help their growing daughters when, for example, their periods start. Barbara described her son's problems with shaving:

> I said to him, 'how about having a good shave' now he's eighteen, and he said, 'Mum, I don't like shaving properly, I'm frightened in case I cut myself,' and I thought, well that's rather silly, he should have gone into shaving naturally by watching his father.

They may also be concerned that their children do not get enough opportunities to learn how to get on with adults of the opposite gender. They fear that boys brought up in a strongly 'masculine' household will not be able to make good relationships with women in adult life or that girls who do not have a consistent father-figure will be unable to sustain relationships with men. There is very little research evidence which sheds any real light on such worries. It is probably more helpful to concentrate on ways of making sure that both you and your children get plenty of adult company; such fears are one good reason amongst many for making every effort to ensure that children do not lose contact with their other parent.

Sometimes change and upheaval force parents to question many of their beliefs about the necessary ingredients of a normal happy life. As they find themselves having to rely on neighbours, friends and, perhaps, more distant relatives, they become increasingly aware of the existence of networks of sharing, love, support and mutual help which cross the boundaries of family and household. As a result their children's lives are enriched by contacts with a variety of adults, some of whom will undoubtedly have a lasting and positive influence on their lives.

THE NON-CUSTODIAL PARENT

No one has yet made a comprehensive study of what happens to parents and children after divorce but a number of different pieces of research indicate that perhaps half of all parents without custody – mostly, but not exclusively, fathers – lose contact with their children within a few years of separation.[19]

Non-custodial mothers face special problems. It is still very unusual for mothers to decide that their children would be better off with their father and custody is normally only given to a father if his wife deserts him, leaving him in charge of their children. Many people still believe that children's ties with their mothers are naturally much stronger than those with their fathers, and mothers who leave their children therefore experience much greater social disapproval than fathers who do so. As a result, such mothers often feel so guilty about what has happened that they find it easier to cut themselves off from their children completely.

Many of the custodial fathers in the Sheffield study had very ambivalent feelings about their ex-wives' contacts with their children. Although they found it hard to understand how any woman could abandon her children and why the children now appeared to be so unimportant to her, they were anxious that, if she reappeared and began to take an active part in their lives once more, her potentially stronger claim to custody as their mother would eventually prevail. As a result, they did not usually encourage their ex-wives' visits. They sometimes justified what they were doing with a belief that no normal mother would have left her children in the first place. Women who are facing such difficulties and who also have to deal with their own guilt and sense of failure about leaving their children will probably find it helpful to talk to others in similar circumstances. MATCH, Mothers Apart from their Children, provides a self-help and advice service for them (see Appendix 2).

There are many reasons why divorced fathers lose contact with their children. Sometimes the battle is lost in the first few months. Ex-wives often discourage visits immediately after separation because they cannot bear to meet the father again or because they feel the children need time to settle down. The children themselves may not appear to enjoy their time with their father and are often very upset afterwards, and in this case a gradual withdrawal may seem to be the only solution.

Whether we are directly involved ourselves or trying to help and support other divorced parents as they face such problems, we need to try to be as open, receptive and perceptive as possible to *both* parents' points of view. For whatever reason, the gulf between them has become sufficiently wide for them to consider that their partnership is over and yet their children are tangible reminders of their continued relationship as parents. They find it impossible to live together but they will have to find new ways of working together if their children are to enjoy a real relationship with their other parent.

In the first months of separation, the custodial and the visiting parent are likely to see access visits and their ex-partner's role very differently. The parent with custody is only too aware of the demands and responsibilities of bringing up children alone in the early months of separation. Learning to cope with unfamiliar domestic problems, as well as trying to be especially sensitive to the children's needs and problems, leaves the single parent with little time and energy. *She* may feel that her efforts on behalf of *his* children are not recognized by her ex-husband, whose only responsibility seems to be to whisk his neatly dressed and presentable children off for Saturday treats. By contrast, *he* feels frighteningly and uncharacteristically powerless in relation to his children. He is dependent on his ex-wife to organize his contacts with his children. He may feel that she determines every detail of their relationship – for example, whether they can visit his new home, or stay overnight, or meet his new girlfriend. It is up to her to decide whether they are too unwell to visit or interpret their wish 'not to see daddy this week'. In addition, he may also feel that, although he is working to keep his ex-wife and children in greater comfort than he enjoys himself, no one recognizes his needs, especially his desire to see his children regularly. Let us consider a divorced mother's possible feelings about access visits in more detail and then focus on the visiting father's experiences and point of view.

Being a parent means taking responsibility for everything which happens to your children. As the complete dependency of babyhood gives way to growing maturity and autonomy, parents are expected to be there, constantly in the background, setting limits, providing support and even a safety net when necessary. The divorced parent may feel she bears this heavy burden alone and that

75

she is at least partly responsible for what has happened to her children. In the first months after separation she may watch them particularly closely, organizing their lives so as to avoid stress and pain. If they are upset when they return from outings with their father, her first instinctive reaction is to protect them from the source of this distress. If she is still very angry with her ex-husband, perhaps because he appears to have settled down very quickly in a new partnership, it is all too easy for her to turn this legitimate concern for her children's feelings into an opportunity to hurt and punish their father. If he left her suddenly it is not surprising that she clings fiercely to those aspects of her life which remain in her control. As the weeks pass by and she is with them constantly, she becomes increasingly confident that she knows what is best for them. Whenever children cry and are obviously upset, we try to comfort them, reassuring them that we will try to get rid of whatever is making them sad, so what is more natural than to suggest that contact with their father is not 'good' for them? It is hard for many divorced mothers to appreciate that they cannot shield their children from the pain of losing a parent who has formerly been an essential element in the security of their daily life. Perhaps the best we can do to help children of any age who face this kind of loss is to share their sorrow, giving them 'permission' to grieve for the past and the opportunity to discover that, for both children and adults, the experience of joy and sorrow are closely related:

> When you are joyous, look deep into your heart and you shall find it is only that which has given you sorrow that is giving you joy. When you are sorrowful, look again in your heart and you shall see that in truth you are weeping for that which has been your delight.[20]

Mothers who have custody of their children and who remarry immediately, or even some time after their first marriage ends, are often very concerned about re-creating an ordinary, normal family life for their children. Several of the remarried couples in the Sheffield study felt that continuing contact with their children's other parent had disadvantages if they were particularly anxious to set themselves up as 'a normal family' amongst their neighbours and friends. Making arrangements about visits provided constant reminders of a past they would have preferred to forget and they often complained that their own attempts to plan joint family activities – days out in the car, holidays, sporting activities – were frustrated by last-minute cancellations and alterations in arrangements. In addition, stepfathers, who saw themselves as giving their wives support in bringing up their children, were inhibited by the shadowy presence of the natural father. If the new family still lived in her old home the botched double-glazing her ex-husband had put in three years ago, the stepson's inherited skill at sports and the stepdaughter's expensive bicycle, a present from her father, would all act as powerful reminders of the ex-husband's continuing presence in their lives.

The strength of such feelings should not be underestimated. To face them requires honesty, courage and, on occasion, a sense of humour, but to do so brings its own rewards. Weekends when the children are with their father become a time when the new couple can concentrate on one another; they could even replace the double-glazing together if it irritates them, secure in the knowledge that someone else is spending two hours in the rain watching the son's football match.

Divorced mothers who do not form a new relationship may find their children's visits to their father particularly hard to cope with because they are afraid they will come into contact with new partners or girlfriends. If their marriage has ended as a direct result of this new relationship, there is sometimes an obscure fear that the woman who has taken away her husband might steal the children's affections as well. She may feel that, exhausted and depressed and still on her own, she is poor company for her children, while her ex-husband's fulfilment in his new partnership makes him a more attractive companion. Access visits may make this situation worse, as it is the custodial parent who usually copes with the day-to-day routine of school, work, rushed meals and early bed, leaving weekends and holidays as the most common times for the children to be with their father.

Understandably, mothers sometimes test the power which custody gives them by insisting that their children do not meet their father's partner. This causes problems for everyone. If the father and his new girlfriend are living together it becomes difficult for him to take his children home, and their times together have to be limited to trips to the pictures and meals out. Longer overnight visits which would give their mother a change and rest and would involve him in ordinary routines with his children are impossible unless he asks his girlfriend to disappear for a night or two, a request which is likely to put a strain on any new relationship. If he defies his ex-wife's wishes he risks losing access altogether and puts his children under an unnecessary strain if they feel they have to edit their accounts of what happened when they stayed with their father. There are no easy answers – workable solutions are only reached when everyone, including the children, exercise some restraint.

In any case, it is reasonable that the children should see their father on his own at first; in the early months after separation, they need to establish a new basis for their relationship with their father now that he no longer lives with them, while he needs to be able to give them his undivided attention, to catch up on their news and the changes in their lives which would be absorbed almost unconsciously if they lived together. They may want to ask difficult questions, or be able to cry and to be naughty in order to test him out. This is more difficult in the company of a stranger who seems to have first call upon his attention. However, children are often very anxious and curious about the details of their other parent's new life. They will want to know where he lives, whether he is happy and who looks after him. Answering such questions inevitably involves the gradual introduction of details about his new partner. If they visit his new place, they will notice whether it seems comfortable and signs of another person will not go unobserved. Meanwhile if these shorter visits seem to be going well, if the children are returned promptly without being overfed or obviously spoilt, then the mother may feel sufficiently secure to agree to a longer visit which would include meeting his girlfriend, especially if it is clear that the children will have plenty of time on their own with their father. In real life it rarely works out so smoothly. Most divorced mothers feel considerable panic when they first face up to their children's growing relationship with their father's new partner and they may begin to make difficulties about access once again. Others place a great strain on their children by using them to find out more about this other person whom they may never have met but who has had such an extraordinarily powerful effect on their lives. It is not surprising that the children of divorced parents are so often characterized as having unusual skills of tact and diplomacy. While such virtues can safely be encouraged – tactfulness is, after all, learning to put the feelings of others first – it is not good for either parents or children, if the children are asked to tell deliberate lies to protect one of their parents. There is a world of difference between a father's gently indicating to his children that their mother might not want to hear very many details about his second wife's new baby and his asking his children to deny that they have met his girlfriend and to edit their stories accordingly.

It is not only children who face anxieties about separation in the aftermath of a family break-up; many parents live with the fear, real or imagined, that their ex-partner will not return the children at the end of an access visit. Such fears, fuelled by the increasing number of 'tug-of-love' stories in the newspapers, sometimes strengthen a custodial parent's desire to sabotage the arrangements for access made by the courts. It is better to face such anxieties openly, even if it means confronting your ex-partner with them, rather than pushing them to the back of your mind.

Many divorced fathers face difficulties in sustaining an active and realistic relationship with their children especially if the children are quite young, because they have had very little to do with their children even before the family split up. As a result, they do not have a strong basis of shared interests and experience on which to build.

Fathers of very young children often find access visits very difficult to organize, especially if it is impossible to take them to his new home. When ideas for trips to the zoo, museums and parks have run out, and the weather turns cold, it is easy to lose heart. It may be better for fathers of very young children to see them when they are with their grandparents for the day or spending time with close friends.

Fathers who are only allowed to see their children for very short periods when they visit their ex-wife's home may find these occasions so awkward and painful, especially if their wife has remarried, that their visits become more and more infrequent.

Breaking Even

Fathers sometimes stop seeing their children as a direct result of their failure to pay maintenance. Although there is no formal connection in law, they feel that their right to access is linked to being able to support their children. Many people believe that being able to provide children with a satisfactory standard of living is an important aspect of being a good father. When they feel guilty about being in arrears with maintenance or have run out of excuses for not paying, they avoid further questions from their ex-wife about money if they do not visit their children. Several fathers in the Sheffield study also told us that when their ex-wives remarried they suggested that they would be prepared to forgo maintenance for the children if the fathers would give up visiting.

Even divorced fathers who are strongly committed to maintaining a lasting relationship with their children and who are actively encouraged to do so by their ex-wives find that they are affected in ways they had not expected and that the pain of not being available to be a 'proper' father is almost more than they can bear. Children take for granted that their parents are both constantly at hand to answer questions, provide food and clothing, settle arguments, 'kiss it better', mend toys or lay down the law, so that parents who are not immediately available, for whatever reason, often feel very guilty. Keith, one of the divorced fathers we spoke to for the radio programmes, had become increasingly aware that although he saw his son Scott regularly they were not as close as when they had lived together. He related how, one Saturday when he went to see Scott, he found that the chain had come off Scott's bicycle earlier in the week and he was full of remorse that Scott had not been able to use his bike for several days simply because his father had not been around to mend it. He described his attempts to compensate for not being a 'proper' father:

> You tend to spend more on them. You spoil them to make up for not seeing them. You want, need their love and it's the only way you can satisfy yourself you can still do something for them without actually being at home . . . He's getting further and further away because he's getting less dependent on me.

Divorced fathers also miss the small pleasures of life at home

80

with their children, watching their progress and sharing unselfconsciously in the rituals of their daily life. As a result, weekend visits are eagerly anticipated and carefully planned, so that everything will work out exactly right, with none of the minor conflicts or inevitable patches of boredom which characterize 'ordinary' family life. As Keith explained:

> You think if you scold him or tell him off in any way you won't see him next week. He might say, 'I don't want to see daddy next week.'

When I talk to parents who have split up about their continuing responsibilities as parents I usually ask them if any of their friends are coping well with the problems which seem to loom so large for them. Even if they cannot think of anyone immediately, they often begin to look out for others in similar circumstances. It is comforting to find that many of the conflicts and misunderstandings of the first few months diminish and that it is not uncommon for parents who have been divorced for some time to say that they now get on much more easily than they did when they were married to one another.

It is also helpful to consider the sort of relationship and pattern of visiting you are aiming for in the long run. It is clear from Wallerstein and Kelly's research (see Appendix 2) that, after five years of separation, many of the children they studied wanted to see their fathers more frequently than they actually did. Many of them would also have preferred to have had more say in the timing and length of their visits to their non-custodial parent, rather than having to fit in with arrangements their parents had made.

Ideally, parents need to set up a pattern of contact which is consistent and relatively predictable and which helps to allay the initial insecurities of all concerned. However, it is also important that the children should be able to contact their non-custodial parent themselves if they are old enough, so that their relationship is not entirely encapsulated within the fixed period of an access visit. A nine-year-old boy whom I met travelling alone on a train proudly showed me a set of stamped addressed letter-cards his

81

father had given him to use whenever he just felt like saying hello, or wanted his father to telephone.

'Have you used any yet?'
'Only once, but I always know they are there.'

When both parents still live reasonably close to one another, children may begin to take arrangements into their own hands, popping round for advice about homework or simply to see what is going on. Sometimes ground rules are needed if they do not tell anyone where they are going or if they are obviously playing one parent off against the other.

It is often convenient for visiting parents to see all their children together, but this is not always welcomed by the children themselves. Every parent of more than one child has on occasion been battered and defeated by the manifestations of the jealousy and rivalry which well up from time to time and children of divorced parents are certainly not exempt from such moods. Anxious to assert their individuality, to claim privileges they believe to be attached to their particular age, or simply to talk quietly on their own, they search for the chance of being alone with Dad during the short time they are together each week. If they are free to come and go between the two homes they are much more likely to be able to bask in their father's undivided attention for a while when they need it.

Informal arrangements of this kind are obviously not possible when parents live some distance apart. Visits have to be planned some time ahead and often involve a good deal of travelling for one or both parents. Although it seems obvious that fathers who cannot see their children very often should try to arrange to have them to stay for longer periods, this can create difficulties for everyone. Some fathers may not feel capable of looking after their children on their own for more than a couple of nights. If they have new partners then ex-wives tend to discourage longer visits and the children themselves may be reluctant to leave the familiar routines of home, their pets and their friends for very long. Nevertheless, it is best if such visits are sufficiently long for everyone involved to stop trying hard to be on their best behaviour, so that there are opportunities to fall out and recover, to scold children if necessary and to make friends again. If possible these visits should encompass ordinary everyday life as well as holiday-times, so that the children can take responsibility for domestic chores and go to bed early occasionally as well as being feasted and entertained.

Parents sometimes worry about the way differences between their two homes might affect children who spend time in both, especially if one parent is much more strict than the other. A single mother who feels she is always battling to control her growing children, may feel that her efforts to set high standards of behaviour are being undermined by her ex-husband when their children stay with him. It is worth trying to work out a common policy over important issues, but it is also necessary to remind ourselves that we do not usually worry much when they spend a weekend with friends whose parents have very different standards to our own. As they grow into adolescence and beyond, developing a tolerant understanding of the variety of ways in which adults organize their lives and the ability to work out their own standards will become an increasingly important part of growing up.

IS IT REALLY WORTH ALL THE PAIN AND DIFFICULTY?

It is impossible to give an answer to this question which would apply to all divorced parents and children, but this chapter ends on the assumption that it is always worth trying to ensure that children do not lose contact with either of their parents after divorce.

Wallerstein and Kelly's evidence suggests that, whether they were still in contact or not, fathers still influenced their children's thoughts and affected their feelings five years after separation; they give a powerful picture of children retaining great loyalty to their absent parent despite many setbacks and disappointments.

Once parents have decided to split up they set in train a series of events and changes which are bound to cause pain and to diminish the quality of their children's lives for a time but, despite the difficulties, the loss of one of their parents is not inevitable. Many thousands of divorced parents from all walks of life are learning to cooperate as parents after their marriage is over. To do so is to lay the foundations of a relationship which may initially be difficult and restricted, but which has the potential to develop and flourish to meet the needs of the children as they grow older and face the future with the support of *both* parents.

CHAPTER 4

Building Afresh:
New Relationships and Partnerships

Splitting up and forming new partnerships, divorcing and marrying again, are now inextricably connected in our society; most of those who divorce eventually remarry or form new domestic partnerships, many within a very short time after splitting up. Generally, the longer a person remains unmarried after divorce, the less likely (s)he is to remarry at all. While some people who never remarry regret this very much – they would like to be part of a couple again but are unable to find suitable partners – others remain unmarried by choice.

On the face of it, we would expect newly separated or divorced people to be reluctant candidates for new partnerships; they have found marriage such a painful, destructive and embittering experience that they were prepared to submit themselves, and their children, to the further trials of separation and divorce. Why do people so often remarry, and what does it tell us about the particular joys, preoccupations and pitfalls of second partnerships?

AN UNBROKEN PASSAGE
FROM ONE PARTNERSHIP TO THE NEXT?

Some marriages come to an end only when one or, more rarely, both partners wish to marry someone else. As we saw in Chapter 1, although it is unusual for affairs of such seriousness to blossom entirely out of the blue, the common phrase 'falling in love' conveys the bewildering sense of powerlessness felt by those who suddenly find that their deepest feelings are aroused. If the partners have simply grown apart, without conflict or violent arguments, they

Breaking Even

may still feel warm affection for each other. A woman may admit to her husband that although she still loves him, she is 'in love' with someone new. Those of us not currently madly in love can survey it all in a balanced, detached manner; we say that such feelings do not last and that they are a poor basis for making serious and potentially costly decisions. Solicitors tend to be particularly world-weary in this respect and they sometimes try to dissuade their clients by telling them bluntly that they cannot afford a divorce. Such advice is generally ignored by those caught in the web of sharply contrasting emotions – the sense of well-being associated with being in love, and feelings of panic and indecision – that their new relationship has brought in its train. Falling in love tends to heighten our sense of our own individuality – we assert that our feelings are different and unique, and that we must work out the consequences for ourselves.

Being in love means different things to different people. Some people fall in love regularly, treating their propensity to do so with amused detachment; it gives an added spice to life and is a potential source of pain or disappointment but is not necessarily to be taken very seriously. Consider, by contrast, the man or woman who has married the first person they ever really fell in love with. As they look back over the past, seeking to explain their lives, falling in love with their spouse was a critical event which has shaped much of their lives since then; it has been the foundation of their partnership, the first step towards parenthood and a source of their most carefully kept memories. Although the circumstances of their partnership may have changed considerably they may still talk of being in love with their partner, even if it is hard to say what this really means or how it shows itself. When they find themselves falling in love again, they will find it much more difficult to weigh up what it means and how they should respond.

This sense of powerlessness, of being unable to do anything but respond to such strong and rarely experienced feelings is heightened if decisions have to be taken prematurely. Margaret, a teacher in her mid-thirties, with two children, then aged twelve and ten, told me how she fell in love with another teacher, Derek, whom she met at a residential course. She went on seeing him secretly for several months:

86

I think now, I was trying to put off making any decision until the summer holidays, so when my husband just came out and asked me whether I was having an affair, I didn't know what to say. I denied it straight away, but somehow we both knew I was lying and I told him a couple of days later. He took some leave from work and when he came back he issued this sort of ultimatum. Either I left home straight away or he would tell my parents – who are very straight-laced – and the head teacher of the school where I worked then. I hated him so much for that it gave me the strength to pack a few things and go. I went straight over to Derek's. Of course he was overjoyed.

Although she returned home for a short period some months later, they did eventually divorce, but when she looks back on that time she still seems rather ashamed and ill at ease about what happened.

In triangular relationships the one in the middle, who is in transition from one relationship to another, may also experience pressure from his/her lover, sufficient at times to constitute a kind of blackmail. The lover, anxious and insecure, afraid that feelings of loyalty and commitment to family will come in the way of their new-found happiness, may try to force their partner's hand by threatening to end the relationship. Although the victim of such pressure may respond by reaching a decision and even acting upon it, it will be very different in its consequences from the kind of decision reached by a person who has had the opportunity to think out and accept responsibility for the longer-term consequences. Important decisions should not be hurried, even by the person making them, and this is very hard for all those involved.

Magazine story images of falling in love, leading to getting married associate marriage with new beginnings, the wedding marking 'the first day of the rest of your life'. Those who remarry are rarely able to mark the beginning of their partnership in this way. Just as it is difficult to decide when a marriage is really over, it is also hard for divorcees to determine when their new domestic partnerships really begin. In future years, there may be some confusion about which anniversaries to celebrate – where, for example, a couple starts living together and then, as commonly happens, one of them later returns home for a period, to give their marriage a final try. A friend once told me how she had read through the prayer book marriage service on the morning her partner moved in with her, a date she remembered easily many years later. The transition was more complicated for her partner, a married man, who had recently left his wife and children. For years he remained uncertain where he belonged. For example, when he was asked his address he would sometimes without thinking give one long out of date, the last place where he remembered feeling happy with his wife. Like many other people in similar circumstances, they began living together with differing and confused feelings about who they were and where they were going. Further confusion will follow when the new partners begin to present themselves as a couple to the world outside.

Despite the fact that many people now openly live together without being married and that such partnerships enjoy a much greater measure of public acceptance than they used to, some couples still choose to present themselves as being married from the moment they start living together. Some may simply not bother to challenge the assumption made by strangers that they *are* a married couple, but for others it involves a much more positive attempt to create the joint identity as a married couple for which they both long and for which one or both of them has endured the pain of ending an earlier marriage. Such deception creates its own strains. Even when they move to a new area where they are unlikely to meet people from their previous lives, they find themselves editing their conversation and constructing elaborate explanations for incongruous elements of their different pasts. If they cut themselves off from their families and former friends in order to pass as married, they may become very isolated, constantly afraid of some unhappy reminder of the past, longing for the day when, the legal formalities complete, they can make it official. Such eager anticipation of a time in the future when, safely remarried, all their problems will be over, can actually prevent them from facing the difficulties endemic to their situation. At a personal level one or both of them has had little or no opportunity to come to terms with the end of their previous marriage if they feel they should always be acting like young lovers or even newly-weds while knowing that they have sacrificed much and caused other people a good deal of pain for this new relationship. It is very important for them to reassure one another that it *is* succeeding and it is particularly difficult for them to face up to misunderstandings, conflicts and potential sources of disagreement. Disappointment and disillusion follow when they find that the open communication and mutual understanding which drew them together in the first place appear to be diminishing very rapidly.

In such circumstances, it is worth trying to explore these problems and, in particular, the recent experiences of the partner in transit. Though deeply in love, he (or she) may be desperately confused by a welter of conflicting feelings about the new partner and the family he has just left behind. Although he feels the joy and elation of being in love, in starting a new phase of life with a partner who appears to meet his deepest needs, their life together is unfamiliar and sometimes beset with problems. It is also hard for him to envisage the future very clearly because there are so many unresolved issues to deal with and difficult hurdles, such as the divorce, to surmount. We may cherish hopes of a satisfying and fulfilling relationship with a life-partner who is able to understand and accept us completely and thus meet all of our deepest emotional needs, but in practice things do not always work out like this. While many couples do eventually enjoy such a close and exclusive relationship, intimacy of this kind grows slowly, based on shared experience and very gradual recognition and exploration of each other's strengths and weaknesses. If one of the participants in a new domestic partnership is still emotionally, legally or financially in transit from one relationship to another, they may *both* find it very difficult to help and support one another as they would want to because so many of the problems and preoccupations of the partner in transit appear to threaten and undermine the relationship, making the future seem particularly uncertain.

Their problems include taking the necessary legal steps to end the previous marriage, sorting out the finances and, if there are children, laying the foundations of a continuing parental relationship with them. As well as being a potential source of guilt and re-crimination, these issues cast their shadow over everyday domestic routines as the couple settles down and makes a new life together.

Jane told me how she had met and fallen in love with Martin, a divorcee and a journalist on a provincial newspaper. Married for some eight years, she had not consciously wanted to start an affair, but she soon began to re-evaluate her own rather staid and conventional marriage to Ian, a wealthy business executive. Much to her regret they had no children and, initially, she felt there was nothing which tied her to her husband. She told him that she was having an affair and left home a few days later. At first she and Martin seemed idyllically happy, and Martin was anxious to get everything settled so that they could marry as soon as possible. Although she had not worked for some years, she took a job and started to build a new life for herself in the town where Martin was based. Her parents took Ian's side and were very upset by what had happened, refusing point-blank to meet Martin. Ian made periodic attempts to get in contact with her but she found herself putting off seeing him to discuss financial arrangements or even returning home to collect the winter clothes she now needed. Martin felt increasingly insecure and, fearing that she might return home at any time, alternated between trying to persuade her to make decisions and asserting fatalistically that it would never work out.

They were living in rented accommodation and they began to look for a house to buy. They would only be able to afford the kind of house they really wanted if she put in the capital from the house she owned jointly with her husband. It looked as if getting this money would take a long time and they wondered whether to buy something smaller in the meantime. Each time they were about to commit themselves to a house she found some unforeseen snag at the last moment. During this time their life was very unsettled, she disliked her work and they quarrelled a good deal over trivial domestic matters. She has now returned to her husband. She still says that she loves Martin very much and that their relationship was always much better than her marriage had been. Martin still finds it hard to reconcile the fact that she constantly compared him so favourably with her husband with her decision to leave.

When a father leaves home to start a partnership with someone new his feelings of loss and of continuing parental responsibility, as well as his contacts with his children, will remain as powerful reminders of a past which can never be completely forgotten. If his new partner has children herself she is likely to understand his feelings much better and the challenge of building a relationship with his new stepchildren may cause him further pain but also bring its own compensations. If his new partner has no children she may find it hard to appreciate the intensity of his guilt and sense of loss. From her point of view, he has chosen her in preference to his wife and the children may seem an unwelcome reminder of his wife's continuing influence on their lives. As they settle down as a couple, establishing new friends, domestic routines and a life-style which reflects what they value in their relationship, she finds that their autonomy as a couple is constantly undermined because of his children. A cosy dinner for two goes cold on the plate when his wife telephones to tell him that one of the children has failed a maths test, plans to go away with friends for the weekend have to be broken when she changes the date of their monthly weekend visit. In the same way that new parents discover how radically their relationship is altered by the arrival of a child, women who begin partnerships with men who are already fathers have to learn how much parental obligations undermine the exclusive mutual commitment which some people regard as ideal in a couple relationship.

CAN IT EVER WORK OUT?

From what has been said so far readers who are involved in a new relationship which overlaps the end of an earlier marriage may be tempted to stop reading and begin packing straight away. We need to remember that many couples *do* successfully transcend such problems and emerge from this period of transition with a sufficiently strong, realistic and accepting commitment to one another to last for the rest of their lives, and also succeed in continuing their relationships with the children, relatives and even ex-partners of the previous marriage. If you find yourself in such a situation and have not yet left your first partner, it might be worth considering the advantages of finding a neutral staging-post, even for a short time, so that you avoid moving, as it is often so graphically and damagingly put, 'straight from one bed to another'. By the same token, both new partners need to pay particular attention to how things seem from the other person's point of view, exercising the kind of tact and restraint which is easier if you allow each other some breathing-space, time to see personal friends or to be on one's own.

STARTING AGAIN: WHO NEEDS A PARTNER?

Not everyone whose marriage ends in divorce falls into a new relationship straight away, but the pressure to remarry or find a new partner can be very strong indeed and is experienced at many different levels. Taxation and welfare systems are organized on the assumption that adults will live in households made up of (married) couples and their dependent children, and any other arrangements are still regarded as a difficult anomaly. While obviously no one will remarry simply to fit in with our current taxation and welfare arrangements, assumptions about the normality of couple relationships are underlined when we come into contact with public officials, who may suggest that problems would be alleviated, or even eradicated, if we were to remarry. Women who are struggling to support and care for their children on their own may be told that their children need the discipline a father would provide or that their tiredness and depression would be relieved by forgetting the past and finding someone new. Instead of encouraging men to learn to cook or to buy a washing machine we urge them to get married again!

In more subtle ways the normality of coupledom is powerfully reinforced in the relationships of everyday life. People on their own feel out of place in social gatherings in which the couple is the usual unit and unaccompanied women often face the additional problem of being regarded as legitimate prey for the marauding advances of men, conveniently able to break out of their own coupledom for a time. Similarly, parents may feel that their children are being stigmatized because they are known to come from a one-parent family and so may look to remarriage to restore a normal family identity for their children.

At a more personal level, as we have seen, those who have been married often miss the comforts, both material and emotional, of marriage; finding a new partner is the most obvious solution to the particular problems of loneliness and isolation experienced by some newly divorced people.

It is worth reminding ourselves that some people choose not to remarry and that it is not the only, nor necessarily the best solution to the problems of divorcees with or without children, and that we should be aware of the danger of pressing this solution upon ourselves or others. One of the real benefits of the rapid changes in patterns of family life that we have seen in the last decade is that a wider variety of possible partnerships, household arrangements and family groupings is becoming increasingly common, thus weakening, albeit very slowly, our conviction that marriage and a two-parent household is the only healthy and natural environment for partnership and bringing up children.

FINDING A NEW PARTNER

Sooner or later many divorced people left on their own begin to think about the possibility of meeting someone new. When all their energies have hitherto been concentrated on survival, the decision to get out more and start mixing again marks an important step towards recovery, signifying growing confidence and a greater sense of self-worth. They may begin to take greater care with their appearance and, where they can, to spend a bit more on clothes and entertainment. Friends and relatives, or even children, may take a hand, persuading them to put the past behind them and to consider remarriage. Parents with custody of children often have the greatest difficulties in finding new partners because they frequently lack the time, energy or money to go out much. They may resort to more formal means of meeting potential new partners, singles clubs of various kinds, marriage bureaux or advertisements placed in the personal columns of local newspapers or periodicals. There is often some sense of stigma attached to using such channels. Many people seem to believe that the most eligible and attractive candidates for marriage find their new partners 'naturally'; formal methods are used only by those who are less eligible in some way or another. But this is not necessarily true.

Breaking Even

MARRIAGE BUREAUX

The proprietors of marriage or friendship bureaux and dating agencies are anxious to dispel this 'less-eligible' image of their clientele and point out that, for instance, many professional people use their service only because they are too busy to waste time on the kind of leisure pursuits and social events at which many people meet their partners. Recognizing the potential stigma attached to meeting through a marriage bureau, some bureau managers suggest that their successful clients should tell their friends and family that they have been introduced by a mutual friend.

The rising divorce rate has stimulated the growth of such agencies, some of which do exploit the lonely and potentially vulnerable. There are few restrictions governing their operation and you should check on an agency carefully before you fill in their application forms or pay them any money. There are three important considerations to bear in mind. You need to be assured that your application will be treated in confidence and in a businesslike manner; that the agency is sufficiently large and well-established to have recruited enough clients to allow good matching of age and background; and that its interviewers have sufficient skill and experience to give you some potentially promising introductions, or to deal with any difficulties which might occur. Generally speaking, small local bureaux, especially if they have not been in business very long, are less likely to meet these standards than the big-name national bureaux with more clients on their books and a greater reputation to lose should anything go wrong. These larger national bureaux also tend to restrict their membership only to those who are already free to marry.

SINGLES CLUBS

Singles clubs of various kinds offer an immediate opportunity of meeting other people in the same circumstances, some of whom are consciously looking for new partners. Some, like Gingerbread groups, cater especially for lone parents while others open their membership to all kinds of people, excluding only those who are currently married. The club activities are usually organized in a way

94

which encourages people to mix and to talk to strangers, so that they can make new friends away from the obvious 'pick-up' atmosphere of a bar or night club. As one of the women in the Sheffield study, who met her second husband at such a club, put it:

> I needed to get out of myself and to do something different and yet it's something I had never done . . . gone out on my own . . . I couldn't do it even though I'd got a lot of confidence . . . walk in a pub and stand there, I felt as if I were there to be picked up. The club gave me that somewhere to go where there were women on their own and they weren't there to be picked up. Everybody sort of chats together and anybody can join in.

Many of the people who go to a club of this kind in Sheffield have no intention of marrying again, but appreciate the varied activities and social life it offers. At the Christmas party last year a number of people told me of their plans to spend Christmas day with one or two others they had met at the club, glad that they would not be spending the day alone again. There are also valuable exchanges of skill when volunteers are called for to mend a washing machine, make curtains or teach someone the first steps in gardening or wine-making. Periodically engagements are announced or marriages celebrated. If this sometimes causes jealousy it is not obvious; most people are quick to share in the good fortune of others and to wish them well for the future.

ADVERTISING FOR A PARTNER

It is surprising the number of people who, whatever their current marital status, glance covertly at the 'friendship' advertisements in the personal columns of newspapers and magazines. They seem to exercise a fascination over us despite the fact that many people are ashamed to admit they have even considered placing or answering such an advertisement. Most of the people I have talked to who have done so were encouraged initially by a friend or relative. Mrs Wickham had been very depressed:

> My sister came down every day to see if I were alright and I just told her 'I'm browned off with stopping in . . . I wish I could

find a decent bloke' ... I said, 'If I could get a decent bloke, that'd make me happy.' So it were her idea, she says 'What about all those what put advertisements in the *Champion* what comes round every week?' ... So she wrote it me out and put it in and I paid £2 for having that put in and I got fifteen replies back.

Her second husband's account of replying to this advertisement masks the considerable embarrassment he felt at describing what happened:

I were sat at me mother's one Sunday afternoon, been for me dinner and we all got playing at cards. Me mother's reading the *Champion* and I'd already seen it but I didn't let on. My mother says, er 'it'd suit thee here, lad ... nice young lady' and, you know, all that tripe. I says, 'ay, a load of rubbish'. So I didn't say nowt like but I went home and straight into the cupboard for the writing pad and that's how we met.

A woman with some experience of advertising in this way once described to me how she dealt with the replies. She only contacted those whom she could talk to first on the telephone and usually had several conversations with them before making plans to meet. She felt this helped her to weed out men who wanted only a sexual encounter, as they usually hinted at this in their telephone conversations. She always arrived early when they arranged to meet so that if she didn't like the look of them when they turned up she could slip away without making herself known. Such precautions are probably wise, especially for women, who sometimes unwittingly make themselves vulnerable to the unwelcome attentions of men whom they know very little about. There can be no hard-and-fast rules about such contacts, but it does seem sensible to avoid taking home a complete stranger whom you have only just met or even giving your address until you have found out more about them. You are not being unduly suspicious if you notice that bits of their stories do not fit together. Many women, and perhaps some men as well, have let themselves in for somewhat alarming or merely tedious episodes when they could not get rid of admirers who would not take no for an answer.

DATING AND COURTSHIP:
SEX AND THE SINGLE PARENT

If you are a lone parent with young children, you will only be able to go out on your own if you can find reliable, affordable baby-sitters. Once the partners in the Sheffield study had found one another, most of their courting was done as a family and many references were made to the part their children had played in the development of their relationship. The problems many of them faced in finding the time and privacy necessary to make love were part and parcel of the tensions they experienced between their own personal needs and their responsibilities as parents.

Just as two parents who are bringing up their children together in the same household often arrive at a division of labour where one of them, usually the woman, takes charge of the children, becoming the 'good', 'responsible' and 'reliable' parent, so parents who have separated may unwittingly reinforce this kind of distinction. When a mother is left on her own with custody and daily care of her children, she often strives even harder to become the ideal parent, constantly sacrificing her own needs to those of her children, as she offers them consistent daily care, encouragement and discipline. By contrast, she, and others, may cast her husband as the 'bad' parent; he has forsaken his children and returned to the carefree ir-responsibility of a bachelor life. He may thus adopt the role of the 'bad' parent by often turning up unexpectedly; he feeds his children junk food and when they are with him every day seems like a holiday. In keeping with this image, he makes no secret of his new girlfriends, while his ex-wife feels that she must protect her children from the evidence of her own need for adult companionship, physical closeness and the opportunity to let go. Thus, full-time and visiting parents may develop very different ways of dealing with the problems of balancing their own needs and their parental respon-sibilities, some of which spring from trying to live up to – or in the father's case, down to – the image they have of themselves as separated parents. When some of the full-time parents in the Sheffield study described the early stages of their relationship with their second partner their difficulties became all too apparent. Mrs Graham met her second husband at work:

I'd met him, obviously, before he started to come back here
and for quite a while the children accepted this stranger because
he only came perhaps once a week . . . and then towards the end
of that year he was coming a lot more often. They could see that
there was something different. Well, we had just fallen in love.
We were older but we were behaving younger and we found this
hard for the children to accept. You see you do all this before
you have your children, you're sort of on cloud nine for two or
three years and then when you have your children you sort of
simmer down a bit . . . you don't always want to be kissing and
cuddling and being in each other's arms but, you see, we've done
it the other way round.

Mrs Thompson's description of how they dealt with problems of
sleeping accommodation illustrates how carefully such matters are
thought out. When Barry, whom she later married, first moved in
with her and her son Jeremy, they slept in separate bedrooms for
several months as Jeremy had been used to sleeping in the same
room as his parents.

We thought it would upset him because there had been me
and his dad and then for me to live with someone else on the
same basis, that would probably upset him.

Things changed when they were offered a second-hand double bed.
When Jeremy went to stay with his grandparents for the weekend
they decorated the spare bedroom and put his bed in it.

Barry painted some signs on the door, you know, 'Jeremy's
room', and did little funny signs all over it . . . and then we sat
his teddy on the bed and wrote a little note which said 'welcome
to your new bedroom', you know, and put it on the bed. And
I think he was so pleased to see the teddy and all the trimmings
and everything that he quite forgot that he was, sort of, he didn't
feel pushed out so much.

In such circumstances, many full-time parents feel it is important
to manage their adult relationships in a way which affects their
children as little as possible so that, on occasion, their responsibilities and even their children's presence may dampen their

spontaneity and, at times, threaten the very existence of a new relationship. In this, as in other ways, they may also be concerned about what happens when their children visit their non-custodial parent. Many of the apparently harsh edicts issued by mothers who refuse to let their children meet their divorced father's new girl-friend are best understood, at least in part, as attempts to shield their children from some of the ambiguities of contemporary sexual moralities. If a mother with custody experiences a good deal of deprivation and inconvenience in order to set a blameless example to her children, she will find it particularly painful to hear from her children that her ex-husband now sleeps in the same bed as his new partner. Ideally it would be useful if both parents could talk about this, but for obvious reasons this is impossible for most people, at least until some time after they have split up.

There are no simple answers to questions of morality and there would be a good deal of disagreement amongst any group of 'experts' or, indeed, amongst divorced parents themselves on such issues. The couples in the Sheffield study, as well as others to whom I have talked since, showed an enormous range of responses. At one extreme divorcees who are waiting to remarry do not live together until it is all legal, primarily in order to set a good example to their children. Others see no harm in welcoming their small children into a bed which also contains a stranger whom the children have never met. If you feel you need to arrive at general principles or have to make a specific decision, perhaps you need to think about the effects of such disclosures on all those involved, including yourself. For example, are your children likely to view the new occupant of the right-hand side of your double bed as a potential step-parent? (Have they been asking you about getting married again? Have they ever been aware of anyone staying the night before? Does their other parent ever have someone 'sleeping in' and what does it signify to them?) If you have been going out with someone for some time and have always refused to let them stay and be seen in bed by the children, what will (s)he infer from this shift in policy and practice? Last but certainly not least, your best guide is whether *you* would feel comfortable about it, because in this, as in other matters, your children are likely to take their cue from you. The specific issue of your children seeing you in bed together is related to other family routines and practices. For example, families differ greatly in their feelings about nakedness, how much parents and children of different ages touch and cuddle and whether children are encouraged to join their parent(s) in bed in the middle of the night or early morning. If the issue continues to loom large it is probably because there are also weightier and more complex issues at stake which also need to be explored.

BECOMING A STEP-PARENT

Throughout history step-parents have had a bad press. Many myths, legends and fairy stories have step-parents as their anti-heroes and -heroines. At best the step-parent is portrayed as unfair and, at worst, as downright cruel and sadistic. Such negative stereotypes persist and were mentioned by many of the step-parents in the Sheffield study. As one stepfather explained:

> The word I don't like is stepfather ... I think it's a terrible word, that.

When he has to fill in official forms, he puts:

> 'Father?' 'Yes', and then they send it back and say 'Are you guardian or step-parent?', that you're not their real father ... you know what I mean. All this ... it's like explaining to everybody all the time, like when you are in a queue and at the back everybody's listening in.

Many step-parents resent the assumption that they are less committed to their stepchildren than natural parents or that relationships in a step-family are necessarily more complicated or prone to conflict. Many of the couples in the Sheffield study spoke with pride of the way their remarriage had enabled them to re-create an ordinary family life for one or both sets of children, often with the addition of a child or children of their new marriage to 'bring everyone together'. However, there was a significant number of remarried couples in the study whose attempts to rebuild their family life had been frustrated by the emotional and material legacy of their previous marriages, which affected both parents and children. In addition some of those who now felt stable and secure had experienced some difficulties with their children when they first started living together.

In our research on step-relationships we quickly learnt that, although step-families share some common experiences and potential difficulties, they come in many different shapes and sizes; new families are formed with children of various ages and adults who have differing experiences of marriage and parenthood. When we talked to the parents in the Sheffield study about their reasons for remarriage, many of them described wanting to re-create a more 'normal' home environment for their children within a two-parent household so that, in part at least, they were motivated by a desire to give their children daily contact with a mother or father figure. Living in an ordinary family of two adults and dependent child(ren) also seemed to make it easier to enjoy the kind of family-based activities and stimulation enjoyed by their schoolfriends living in unbroken families. Suffice it to say that, just as in the long run 'staying together for the sake of the children' may not be in their best interests, neither would a second marriage entered into primarily in order to provide them with the missing parent and a 'normal' family.

It was clear, however, that many of the couples in the Sheffield study had placed a great deal of emphasis on how well their children got on with potential new partners. While prospective new partners try to gain the children's approval, their parent wonders anxiously whether her/his children reflect their qualities and achievements as a lone parent. Early encounters can be very fraught; everyone is trying too hard and children of all ages have their own ways of recognizing and responding to an atmosphere which suggests that the adults supposedly in charge are themselves anxious and ill at ease. There are no easy tricks for dealing with children, no human equivalents of Barbara Woodhouse's equine nose-blowing. Obviously potential step-parents who have already had children of their own, or some other experience of children, usually find such early meetings easier than people – and there are many of them – who have hitherto lived insulated from day-to-day contact with children. It seems to me that there is a good deal to gain from being, in the transatlantic slang, 'laid back', not off-hand but not gushing either. If you wait until the children make the first approach, and then give them your undivided attention, realizing that they will probably want to return to their own preoccupations and friends quite quickly, this is a better foundation than the patronizing, half-interested talking-down inflicted on children by some who have hitherto had little to do with children. An early meeting with the fourteen-year-old son of the man I used to live with included going with him to see the film *Tommy*, an intensely shared but almost entirely non-verbal experience!

STEPFATHERS

For many step-parents in the Sheffield study being able to provide useful skills gave them a passport into their new family. Thus stepfathers, and their wives, spoke proudly of the new family, referring to new clothes and toys and the visits and outings the children now enjoyed. In addition both mothers and stepfathers referred to the advantages of 'having a man around the house', describing their domestic lives together in vivid and enthusiastic detail. Mr Hutchinson, for example, described how his own interests

> ... rubbed off on the lads ... different things, they'll start getting a screwdriver ... and I've no need to ask them if I want anything done in the garden. They *want* to do the garden. The lads have got the same interests as me now.

As her children began to spend more time with their stepfather, Mrs Hutchinson found them easier to handle. Her youngest son was particularly prone to asking 'silly questions':

> I've noticed a big change in him since we've been married, because before that he was ... a demon ... and I couldn't do very much with him at all. If I wanted him to behave I'd just got to keep him in which wasn't very fair, but if I let him out he got up to all sorts of mischief and now he doesn't.

All her children have now begun to ask their stepfather when they want something:

If they want to go out anywhere they don't ask me, they ask him. Usually I'm busy so it's obvious that they'll go to him first. They've got a lot more thoughtful like that ... If I'm doing something they don't come pestering me like they used to. He's really interested and they can tell, he doesn't sort of sit and take it in one ear and let it out the other ... We'll all go to the library, and he'll get all the kids together and he'll help them to look for the book they want.

At the end of the interview she concluded:

I think really they're benefiting more than I am from this marriage [laughs] if you know what I mean. There are more of them for Roger's love to be shared out, but they all seem to be flowering.

STEPMOTHERS

As a society we are much clearer about what we expect of a 'good mother' than a 'good father'. Mothers usually do much more of the daily work involved in looking after and bringing up children as well as taking more responsibility for how they turn out in the long run. It is not simply that mothers are responsible for their own children, but that women generally are assumed to be natural caretakers of children, and when a woman gets involved with a man with children, she may feel that she is expected to become involved in daily child care from a very early stage. She may even, perhaps mistakenly, believe that a man's heart is to be reached through his children. It is hard for most women to avoid the belief that motherhood is both normal, inevitable and a woman's greatest source of fulfilment, so women expect to enjoy caring for children and to be judged by their achievements in this sphere. Thus many potential stepmothers embark on a partnership with a full-time lone father with very high expectations of how they will restore and re-create a satisfying domestic life for their new family.[21] Sometimes such aspirations include more than a touch of implied criticism of how he managed in the past, so that a woman who bursts into her new boyfriend's home and family life with the kind of missionary zeal that encompasses everything from a more hygienic regime for the cats to getting the children to do their homework and brush their teeth regularly may find herself less than welcome. Men who have struggled to rebuild a satisfactory family life for themselves and their children out of the ruins of a broken marriage do not necessarily believe that their family is incomplete without a woman. Like many lone mothers, they may want to share the burdens and pressures of child care as well as what Pasternak described as 'the poetry of the trivia of married life', but they do not want to be thought to be starting a new relationship simply in order to acquire a housekeeper and childminder.

Some of the difficulties of stepmothers who are not mothers themselves originate from their inexperience with children generally or their lack of knowledge about their own stepchildren's past. Women who care for their stepchildren and are regarded as their mothers by the outside world, but have never given birth themselves and know little or nothing of the children's earlier development, clearly have to cope with ambiguities and uncertainties not shared by natural mothers. Having a baby of their own was an important milestone for most of the previously childless stepmothers we spoke to in Sheffield, adding to their stock of experience with children and making the idea of 'motherhood' real to them in a different way. Mrs Parker found she was able to make greater sense of her stepdaughter Emily's earlier development after she had her own child, Ben:

> I knew Emily from when she was three and I don't think I missed out particularly from not knowing her before then, because I think at three the child's personality is pretty obvious, judging by Ben. Anyway they are all pretty much the same as babies, you know.

Anne and Barry met shortly after his first wife, Kirsty, died suddenly and unexpectedly, leaving him to care for his four children. Anne had been working part-time for his wife as a nanny to his youngest daughter but did not actually meet Barry until he contacted her to ask if she could help him with the children. Despite the circumstances and an eighteen-year age difference they became very close and the children grew to rely on their nanny more and more. Within two months, Barry proposed and they were married the same autumn amidst much family opposition. When Anne was asked whether she felt she had missed out through not knowing her stepchildren when they were small, she commented:

> Oh yes, in fact I always say I'm very jealous of Kirsty, that she bore my children, you know [laughs]. OK, I've had one, but it's not the same, but I've got a perceptive sort of imagination ... if an incident was talked about with Barry about when they were children, and it crops up a few years later, I'm *there* knowing it all and if they ask me and Barry's not around I'm able to talk about it quite happily. I mean I had Katherine when she was, what, only eighteen months old and I had Victor when he was about six; I knew those two then and had them to look at, to imagine what the older ones were like when they were little.

Another stepmother, whose stepson was ten when she was interviewed, recognizes some of the irritations of not being with children as they grow and develop:

> He's quite old for his age, and I suppose it's like getting to know another person. He's not a young child that you can gradually get to know as they develop and I think in that respect it's harder ... you know, he's got ideas, set ideas and things like that and it's a case of both of us really adjusting to each other.

COOPERATING AS PARENTS: QUESTIONS OF DISCIPLINE

When we consider the new relationships created by a remarriage involving children, the potential problems of the step-relations seem most immediate, but some of the early difficulties of such new families can be understood best by focusing on the *adults'* differing expectations of parenthood to one or both sets of children. Many of the Sheffield couples described difficulties with children during the first months they lived together. They were establishing new domestic routines, perhaps moving house, and some of the new household might not even know each other very well. Dealing with the children of the family was, at this stage, very much a matter of 'conscious parenthood' and it was clear that many couples spent a good deal of their spare time discussing the finer points of child management. Although most of the couples we spoke to felt that their early difficulties soon passed as the children and their new step-parent became better acquainted and they all settled down together, others continued to have serious problems with their children.

By the time we reach adulthood most of us have acquired views about bringing up children which we add to and modify when we become parents ourselves, so two parents who remarry and start a new family life together already have established beliefs about and experience of managing children, and these two sets of beliefs may not necessarily coincide. Several of the couples in the Sheffield study had differing views about smacking children so that, for example, Michael found himself wincing when his wife punished his stepson, Timothy:

> Timothy can be a little ... Dennis the Menace, you know, but I've seen Jean chastise him and tan him really hard on his backside and I've felt it for him, and I've thought, 'Oh crikey' as if he were my own and I've thought 'Oh Jean, don't hit him', because I don't hit him.

Conflicts over the management of children can cause rifts in any marriage but there are additional complications when step-relationships are involved. In times of stress parents may begin to defend their own children or blame their partner for their step-child's behaviour. Two couples in the Sheffield study were experiencing sufficiently serious difficulties to make them wonder whether they would stay together and the danger signals were the same for both – their quarrels and disagreements over their children were now so out of hand that they were unable to stop themselves arguing in front of the children. Jennifer anxiously described how her second husband, Martin, had said when they first began seeing each other:

> 'I don't like arguing in front of the children' and, if anything,

now he's the one who does it most in front of the children. In fact he doesn't seem to be able to control himself now; if he's got something to say he says it.

Martin readily admitted that he 'flew off the handle' easily:

> If I do correct them I'm probably a bit sterner than what I should be, then Jennifer'll jump down on me and she'll say I wouldn't correct my own like that.

Jennifer summed up many of the problems of newly remarried parents very graphically when she tried to explain why they argued so much about her children:

> I think he could do without the girls altogether. He's accepted them because they were a part of *me* but really I think Martin's all for me, he wants my time all the time and he can't understand why I can't give one hundred per cent of my time. I've got to sew a button on, or I must do this Guide uniform, there's always something. I wish that I could give him one hundred per cent of my time, you know ... I wish that I could have two or three years just enjoying myself with him.

PART-TIME STEP-PARENTS

As we have already seen, remaining an active part-time or, in legal language, a non-custodial parent presents many difficulties and it is not surprising that so many children soon lose effective contact with their part-time parent. If this parent has remarried their new partner will be a part-time step-parent in name only. They are aware of the existence of their partner's children but, on the surface at least, their lives are unaffected by them. For some parents loss of custody and, eventually, any real contact with their children may make them particularly anxious to have further children in their new marriage, an ambition all too often frustrated by one or other partner's earlier sterilization. One of the peculiarities and potential sources of difficulty in second marriages is that partners come together with a variety of earlier experiences of parenthood and may have very different views about having children together, so that reaching a decision may need a good deal of careful and sometimes painful discussion whatever the circumstances.

Part-time parents who do succeed in keeping in close contact with their children deserve all the help they can get from other members of their family and, especially, from their new partner, but they do not always get it. Many part-time stepmothers find the ambiguities of their relationship with their husband's children hard to tolerate and, in addition, the way his continuing responsibilities to his children and contact with his ex-wife disrupt their life together. As in so many areas of family life, it is often trivial and apparently unimportant issues which betray deeper, more painful feelings. For example, there are inevitably areas of uncertainty and insecurity in any new partnership, and the prior claims of one partner's children who visit occasionally and unexpectedly, taking his attention and disrupting the new couple's time together, may make the other partner feel very left out. If, once the feelings of insecurity, rejection or of being misunderstood have subsided a bit, you can both think about it carefully and talk about it to someone else, although not necessarily to each other, if that is difficult, then it will be easier to cope with what is happening. Viewed from the outside it is not surprising that each member of a group of two adults and the children of one of them, drawn together temporarily for an afternoon, a weekend, or a fortnight's holiday as 'an ordinary family', will be unusually insecure. The children separately clamour and compete for the attention of their father, who they may feel they do not see often enough, uncertain whether he still loves and accepts them. His partner, hurt that he seems to be ignoring her, despite earlier protestations of love and commitment, is faced with children whom she hardly knows and who are powerful reminders of a past which seems to interfere with their present and future happiness at every turn. He stands in the middle, uncertain of his children's love, anxious for their visit to go well, but aware that his girlfriend feels unhappy or rejected ... how will he ever get it right?

One way of looking at such problems is to consider how the balance of giving and taking, being strong and being weak should constantly alter between close friends, partners and members of the same family. The word 'should' is important – many relationships become sterile and even destructive because the respective roles have become fixed. One person is imprisoned in a cage of inadequacy and dependence at the expense of the other, who is burdened with the strain of being permanently strong. In working relationships, politics and everyday life, we are used to making bargains based on exchange, some quite clear and explicit, others implied . . . 'If you vote with me on item 6, I'll support you over item 11' . . . 'If you pick up my children from school today, I'll look after yours when you go to the hospital next week.' If allowed to do so, most partnerships flourish on this kind of give and take, especially when both partners have outside interests, commitments and responsibilities which have to be balanced with their loyalty and commitment to one another. Thus, if a part-time stepmother can let her husband get on with maintaining continuing contact with his children unencumbered by feelings of divided loyalty, she will be able to give him help and support where he feels weakest and most threatened. Sharing in getting things ready and in making good meals, being ready to go off and leave father and children together without expecting thanks or attention, are practical ways of demonstrating such support. If this hurts, as it undoubtedly will, the time for her to show weakness is afterwards when it is her turn to be cosseted and supported. If this sounds like a counsel of perfection, remember that this kind of sharing depends on them both having investments and responsibilities outside the partnership – difficulties often arise because women are still encouraged to see coupledom as the entire centre of their existence. At the most practical level, friends, independent interests and projects mean that the stepmother has somewhere to go, allowing the children to have their father's undivided attention for a while.

GETTING IT RIGHT THIS TIME

When people discover that my job has included doing research on second marriage their first question is nearly always 'Do second marriages work out better than first?' For some it is a matter of idle curiosity or academic interest but for others, those who have experienced, or who contemplate, the pain and upheaval of splitting up and then remarrying, their question is tinged by anxiety, so that they can almost be seen crossing their fingers behind their backs.

The official statistics present a gloomy picture; the rapid increase in the number of people remarrying which followed the divorce reforms of the late 1960s appears to have led to a rise in the numbers of divorces involving remarried partners. Present trends suggest that, in general, remarriages are now even more likely to end in divorce than first marriages. However, while two people marrying for the first time are usually relatively similar, remarriage can involve many different combinations and permutations of age and previous experience of partnership, so that some of these pairings may be much more risky than others. For example, remarrying couples who first married when they were very young and are still in their mid-twenties with no children may move on again before they reach thirty, whereas older couples who finally remarry in their late thirties after a long period of uncertainty and upheaval seem, on the face of it, unlikely to be eager to risk going through it all again.

Rather than drawing comfort or a sense of pessimistic fatalism from such statistics, it is better to consider some of the factors which promote or hinder the growth of a satisfying second partnership. The couples in the Sheffield remarriage study differed greatly in the degree to which they had been able to put the past behind them, and this often affected many aspects of their life together as a family. Some of the couples in our study found that their daily lives were still shaped by an emotional and material legacy of the past which they were still unable to get rid of many years later.

Although it is never possible to forget the past completely, and vain attempts to do so are often signs of hidden pain and unresolved anger, we need to face and come to terms with what has happened to us, whatever our circumstances, before we can really make a fresh start. Help to talk about and make sense of the past comes from many sources, friends, our new partner and, on occasion, professional helpers of one sort or another. In times of stress, different and confused bits of our past press very heavily upon us and it may be helpful to talk to a therapist or counsellor. An increasing proportion of work done by local Marriage Guidance Councils now involves people in second partnerships.

It is equally important that divorced people in new partnerships do not make their own and other people's lives unnecessarily difficult by prolonging old conflicts and clinging to legal or financial arrangements which provoke constant and painful reminders of the past. Within limits we all make at least some aspects of our own destiny and there may be a time when it is necessary to admit defeat and 'cut loose', whatever the loss of face involved. There are, however, important differences between disputes about money, property and so on, and conflicts over children.

As we have seen from Chapter 3, there is generally a great deal to be gained from making every effort to ensure that the parent without custody remains in contact with their children. Although it may appear that a battle has been 'won' or 'lost' – according to your viewpoint – when the non-custodial parent withdraws, this may not help the children. Making an emotional separation from an ex-partner, calling a truce but remaining in contact as parents, calls for a great deal of courage, especially if your new partner finds this contact threatening. The more that remarried partners learn to accept each other, especially those who have commitments and responsibilities which remind them of their earlier partnership, the less likely they are to find that the problems which inevitably occur from time to time drive a wedge between them. For many of the divorced parents in the Sheffield study, being able to put their own past behind them and forgive *themselves* helped them to be more tolerant of reminders of their partner's past.

Marge and Mel, who spoke to us for the radio series, began their life together in very difficult circumstances after a long period of pain and uncertainty which affected his ex-wife and his children very deeply. Some years later their life together as a family still had to adapt to the children's visits to their mother and the effects these had on all of them. They spoke very openly and frankly about their feelings, amply illustrating their commitment to make things work out for themselves and their children. They were asked:

Do you feel what has happened will have any lasting effect on the children?

MEL: No, I don't. I think that ... we have brought them up in a way that they could cope with it.

MARGE: I think that we both agree that we would never ever inflict it on them again. I mean in getting married we made the sort of pact – I know, I guess everybody who gets married doesn't expect to get divorced but, we deliberately discussed that, the fact that no way would we ever put them through that again ... and, therefore, we'd work extra hard at our relationship to make sure it doesn't happen again.

CHAPTER 5

Facing the Future

Once they have really faced up to the end of their marriage the next step for most people is to 'put themselves together again' and to make 'a fresh start', alone or in a new partnership. Finding and making a new home, learning to live within new financial limits, organizing and coming to terms with access visits, finding new interests and making new friends are all milestones on the road back to 'getting back to normal'. After comes the unspoken question, 'Well, what's next?', as they begin to face the future. For many divorced people the future stretches ahead with little prospect of change or improvement; even those who have already made new partnerships are often prey to doubts and uncertainties which are particularly difficult to disclose.

Feelings about the future are often highly contradictory. While we relish the security derived from the predictable, ordered continuity of daily domestic life, in fantasy at least, we reach out for adventure, surprise and the opportunity to take risks. In the past most people believed that it was only the young who needed risk and adventure, that when people married and, more particularly, when they had children they settled down into an adult seriousness from which there were only very limited and temporary opportunities of escape for all but the most wealthy and privileged. Recently our ideas and experiences have changed a great deal and many people find their circumstances changing completely unexpectedly when they are well into adult life. Although the shock of being made redundant, the sense of betrayal at the end of marriage, often seem overwhelming at first, I am constantly inspired by people's amazing resilience, their capacity to turn potential disasters to their advantage and fight courageously to begin again. Sometimes redundancy, whether from a job or a marriage, enables people to recognize and express aspects of themselves which had previously been entirely unsuspected or had been given no scope for development.

CONSTANT CHANGE IS HERE TO STAY

A friend gave me a postcard with this message – threat or promise – when it was first announced that the college where we worked would be merged with the local polytechnic. I thought of it again when David Clark and I were reviewing the data from our study of remarried couples. From the time that their first marriages had ended, their lives seemed to have been unusually eventful and some complained quite specifically that they had not been able to settle down again to ordinary life as they would have liked. It is of course impossible to know how many unbroken families actually live lives of unchanging tranquillity; most of us probably underestimate the potential for crisis and change in 'normal' families. Divorcees, especially if they are parents, seem especially vulnerable to unexpected events which seem to threaten either their material or their emotional stability. Consider, for example, an imaginary but fairly typical couple, Howard and Jane, who split up amicably after growing further and further apart for many years. His work took him to a new city but he made sure that he saw his children almost every weekend and for prolonged periods at holiday times. As they had sorted out their finances reasonably satisfactorily on their own they did not see much point in getting a divorce at the time. Howard first became aware that Jane had a new boyfriend three years later when the children mentioned that they had seen a film with 'Pete' the previous weekend. Some weeks later, when he returns the children, Jane produces divorce papers already completed, suggesting casually that it is probably time they 'tidied things up'. Suddenly the delicately balanced relationship with his children and their mother is under attack. He is frightened by the strength of his feelings and he finds it difficult to contemplate the final ending of his marriage and, more significantly, his potential replacement by a new step-parent.

In other circumstances the remarriage of an ex-partner is eagerly anticipated, for it will lighten the burden of guilt for the partner who caused the original break-up. It will also release an ex-husband from his maintenance obligations. When a man leaves his wife and forms a relationship with someone else, the new couple often depends on her earning capacity as well as his, especially if he is paying regular maintenance. Most women in their twenties who are marrying for the first time look forward to having children of their own but their partners, if they have been divorced and have already had children, may be much more uncertain about starting another family – reluctant to go through the nappy stage again, more unsure about the long-term future than they will openly admit, and unwilling to sacrifice their present standard of living. In this case the decision to have children may be delayed until the couple feels more secure; this is sometimes starkly rationalized as not being able to afford children of their own until the ex-wife remarries.

One important source of change – taken for granted when there is nothing amiss – is the growth and development of the children. As divorced parents face the future they are bound to wonder how the divorce will affect their relationship with their children as they grow older. Will children who were too young to understand why their father left home eventually despise him for his disloyalty? Will they blame their mother, who had to cope with years of poverty and struggle on her own, for the austerity and loneliness of their childhood?

Many non-custodial parents, however close and frequent their contact with their children, describe their pain at missing the small but significant milestones of their children's growth and development – a loss they share, incidentally, with parents whose work takes them away from home for prolonged periods of time. In certain circumstances this can have extreme consequences if their relationship with their children remains frozen as it was when the family first split up, fixed in a mould set by the access arrangements made at the time of separation. Wallerstein and Kelly describe this process very vividly:

> It is as if the divorce has caused the clock of the relationship to stand still and child and parent continue ever after, as in a

fairy tale, to perceive each other as each appeared years earlier, and to respond to each other's needs in accord with earlier perceptions and expectations.[22]

CHANGING PATTERNS OF ACCESS

The access arrangements, painfully fought over at the time the split was made, may become increasingly inappropriate as children grow older and everyone's circumstances change, but all three parties – children, mother and father – are reluctant to raise the subject directly for fear of reopening old wounds, losing ground or having to make more concessions. With the passage of time many divorced parents find they can talk more easily together about their children than when they first separated, and as a result find they are making much more flexible arrangements for visiting and allowing the children themselves to have a greater say in the arrangements. When this is not possible, however, the access pattern remains unchanged, and may seem increasingly restrictive to the children. Grumbling, or an outright refusal to see their non-custodial father, may be their way of drawing attention to their needs. If, for example, they want to be free to join a school team which plays on Saturday, to do a paper round or simply to choose for themselves how to spend their leisure, this should not be viewed as a sign that they are rejecting their father entirely. By the same token, children who cling to their visiting parent at the end of a visit, pleading to be allowed to live with them, may simply be making a strong plea for more time with their non-custodial parent and are certainly demanding greater autonomy.

It is not simply the *pattern* of access arrangements which becomes frozen, but also the *relationships* themselves. Children, whatever their family circumstances, reach out for opportunities to demonstrate their greater independence as they grow older, and to have their new skills and growing autonomy recognized. But the visiting parent, lacking the day-to-day contact which would provide countless reminders of their children's growth and development, may continue to treat them as if they were still the age they were when their parents separated. In addition, non-custodial parents rarely have as many opportunities to talk about their children as married parents and consequently have fewer chances to make sense of their children's behaviour and to review their progress. In such circumstances it is worth making a particular effort to find someone – perhaps in similar circumstances – with whom to enjoy indulgent conversations about each other's children, the problems of organizing access and the like!

CHANGES IN CUSTODY

Official statistics and the limited research data on custody implies that most orders made at the time of separation or divorce fix where the child lives until she or he grows up and leaves home and that formal alterations in custody are rare. It is likely that informal changes in custody, as well as temporary alterations in domestic arrangements, are much more common in reality than the figures suggest, and are considered by even larger numbers of parents and children. There are many reasons why such changes take place. Lone mothers may struggle on for some years after separation until their eventual collapse means that their children have to be taken over by relatives, their non-custodial father or into the care of the local authority, either temporarily or permanently. On occasion, changes in their circumstances may lead both parents to reconsider their decision – for example, if the custodial mother intends to travel abroad with a new partner. In addition, one or more of the children may press for a change in custody, sometimes taking matters into their own hands by running away to the other parent without warning. While most children escape at some time into the fantasy of punishing their parent(s) by wrapping their belongings and some Hovis sandwiches in a red-and-white spotted handkerchief and leaving home, many children of divorced parents do actually have somewhere to run to!

Graham, the fourteen-year-old son of parents who had divorced ten years earlier, described for our radio programmes how he ran away from his father and stepmother after a bitter family argument. After spending the night in a telephone box he set off on the sixteen-mile journey to his mother's:

117

When I got about half-way there I began to feel a bit hungry and I passed a big garden with some apple trees with cooking apples on. I reached for 'em and grabbed 'em and rode off a bit fast, looking behind me all the time just to make sure there were no policemen coming after me. I was wondering what our mum was going to say to me . . .

Neither he nor his twelve-year-old sister, Angela, had been getting on well with his stepmother and her children and his flight led to lengthy discussions at a local conciliation service and, eventually, to a change in custody for both him and his sister. Their story illustrates two important issues which arise when custody changes are made some time after parents first separate. First, when the children are older, they are more likely to initiate a change themselves. It is at adolescence that their increasing sense of their identity as individuals gives them the strength to challenge arrangements which no longer seem to meet their needs. It may be particularly difficult for the various parties involved to evaluate and, if necessary, accept what older children are trying to show by behaviour which seems extreme and uncompromising. Secondly, there is an inevitable tension between the concept of brothers and sisters as a single unit – 'the children' – and their needs as individuals. While it is unusual for custody of children to be divided when their parents split up, they may later attempt to alter the custody arrangements individually, and cause a great deal of rivalry and misunderstanding in doing so.

TROUBLES WHICH PERSIST

At least some of the readers of this book will be feeling that its implied message, that eventually most of the problems surrounding splitting up do eventually diminish, is much too optimistic. If they have been separated for some years and are still coping with the poverty and deprivation of single parenthood or the loneliness of living on their own, without any contact with their children, divorce has no compensations and the future appears to hold no possibility of change or improvement. Others are alarmed and dismayed by the lingering scars the past has left on their children. Some, like Job in the Old Testament, can scarcely bring themselves to face another day for fear of some new blow or disappointment falling upon them without warning.

There is very little in my social scientist's briefcase that I can draw out to bring comfort or assistance at this point. When we are in despair we are most likely to feel that no one can possibly understand our plight – and if they do, what help is that? The following comments are not based on any sociological theory, although, in part at least, my understanding of the kind of suffering broken family relationships can cause has been increased by carrying out social research. In this instance I am writing mainly from first-hand experience, and about lessons learned as I listened and held hands with others in distress.

Pain of one kind or another is an inevitable part of human experience and can never be entirely avoided, but this should not prevent us from working to bring about social and political change – to alleviate poverty, for example – nor should it be used as an excuse when we consciously and deliberately inflict pain and suffering on others. Nevertheless, the acceptance of the inevitability of pain may help us to recognize that our suffering is our own responsibility. That is not to say that we have brought it upon ourselves or even that it was a just desert for some earlier failure or misdeed, but rather that there comes a time when we must assimilate the pain – make some stand against it and be prepared to learn what it may have to teach us.

> And a woman spoke, saying, Tell us of Pain.
> And the Prophet said:
> Your pain is the breaking of the shell that encloses your understanding.
> Even as the stone of the fruit must break, that its heart may stand in the sun, so must you know pain.[23]

The first step towards assimilation is often disclosure. If we are locked in a cage of fear and self-pity it becomes increasingly difficult to ask for help or even to admit the intensity of our suffering. Some time ago I was awoken from a menacing dream by the sound of my own voice; 'that hurts,' I heard myself cry out. I switched the light on, searching for security in familiar objects and the usual sounds of the night. Had somebody been trying to hurt me in my dream? At first I could remember very little about it but gradually, tears running down my cheeks, I realized that I had been crying out about a recent, unacknowledged pain, which was the more intense because it echoed earlier occasions when people I had begun to care for suddenly disappeared from my life. In this instance there was little I could do about it, but at least I now knew it was there.

The very recognition that we are wrestling with anxiety and pain sufficient to overwhelm us is a potential source of energy, the energy we need to break out of isolation and search for help. Unfortunately in our late-twentieth-century world the phrase 'seeking help' suggests visits to professionals, a lone pilgrimage through medical, welfare or legal bureaucracies until a 'cure' is achieved. Although there are many problems where professional help is greatly needed, what most of us need first of all is to reach out to someone else who will wait while we try to tell them where it hurts and what we are frightened of. As experts have multiplied, we have steadily lost confidence in our own capacity to support and sustain one another.

When people in distress do reach out and admit that they need help by sharing their pain with someone who will listen to them, they are more likely to make good use of specialist help too. Take, for example, someone who finds they're still submerged by their own grief and depression years after their marriage ended or who is crippled by continuing anxiety about symptoms of distress in their children. If they can talk to somebody about their fears *before* they visit the doctor they will be able to explain more clearly how they feel and the kind of help they need. They will also be less likely to allow themselves to be fobbed off with a repeat prescription for tranquillizers or platitudes about children from broken homes. Similarly, an ex-partner who is smarting under continued legal injustices may gain sufficient confidence to seek legal advice if they find the opportunity to discuss their difficulties with a friend first.

'I HAVE NO ONE TO TURN TO'

Many people have felt at times that there is no one to whom they can confide their troubles, and this is why organizations like the Samaritans were set up. Give them a call – their phone number will be in your local telephone directory. Or you might prefer to write to a newspaper or magazine agony column or make a call to a phone-in advice programme on local radio (Anna and the Doctor on Capital Radio can be strongly recommended if you live in London). It's a start!

WHAT ARE WE WORKING TOWARDS?

Whenever a particular stage or period in our lives is over there are elements of the past which are eventually left behind and others which we carry with us into the future. When couples split up there is a tension between those elements of the past they must learn to put behind them in order to begin again and make a fresh start – alone or in a new partnership – and the elements of their partnership which can never be entirely eradicated. Children are both an obvious reminder of the past and a source of continuing and, hopefully, shared responsibility. Perhaps the greatest challenge of all is to learn how to distinguish these different elements and thus to live fully for the present and to retain some hopes for the future. Setting the past behind us means forgiving ourselves as well as other people, garnishing our memories but not living off them, and making a deliberate end to ancient conflicts which threaten our own, our ex-partner's and our children's present stability. Two thirds of the couples who divorce each year cannot make a clean break because they have continuing responsibilities for their children; they can never put the past entirely behind them, at least until their children grow up.

> Now that my parents have split up they don't seem to be able to talk to each other at all. I'm very worried about this because if I ever do get married I'd like them both to come to my wedding.

(English essay written by an eleven-year-old girl, 1974)

121

APPENDIX 1

Useful Addresses

Action for Lesbian Parents
   4 Trinity Street
   Cambridge
   (Cambridge 66841)
Helps mothers in custody/access cases and gives support and advice.

Association of Separated and Divorced Catholics
   The Holy Name Presbytery
   8 Portsmouth Street
   Manchester
   M13 9GB
   (061-748 6977; 061-969 0741)

Birmingham Association for the Unmarried Mother and Her Child
   Room 42, Dr Johnson House
   Colmore Circus
   Birmingham
   B4 6AL
   (021-236 8911)

Catholic Marriage Advisory Council
   15 Lansdowne Road
   London
   W11 3AJ
   (01-727 0141)

Cherish – An Association of Unmarried Parents
   2 Lower Pembroke Street
   Dublin 2
   (0001 682744)

Child Poverty Action Group
  1 Macklin Street
  London
  WC2 5NH
  (01-242 3225)
Pressure group; gives advice on benefit problems. Will help with tribunal representation.

Chiswick Family Rescue Ltd
  369 Chiswick High Road
  Chiswick
  London W4
  (01-995 2082/5003/4430)
Contact: Tina Wood
Refuges throughout the country where battered women and their children can go.

Cruse (National Organization for the Widowed and their Children)
  Cruse House
  126 Sheen Road
  Richmond
  Surrey
  TW9 1UR
(01-940 4818/9047)

Divorce Action Group
  19 Upper Beechwood Ave
  Ranelagh
  Dublin 6
  (0001 681610, day)

Divorce Conciliation and Advisory Service
  38 Ebury Street
  London
  SW1W 0LU
  (01-730 2422)
Contacts: Hilary Halpin and Patricia Harris
A counselling service on emotional, practical and legal matters which is not free, but a non-profit-making organization, so fees are kept as low as possible.

Families Need Fathers
  37 Garden Road
  London SE15
  (01-639 5362)
A self-help group campaigning for rights of fathers in relation to custody
and access.

Federation of Services for Unmarried Parents and Their Children
  11 Clonskeagh Road
  Dublin 6
  (0001 698351)
Contact: Margaret Dromey

Gingerbread
  35 Wellington Street
  London WC2
  (01-240 0953)
Gen. sec.: Julie Kaufmann
Self-help groups throughout the country.

Haringey One Parent Enterprises
  c/o Devonshire Hill Library
  Compton Crescent
  London N17
  (Liza, 01-801 2589, and Thelma, 01-884 9590)

Jewish Marriage Council
  529B Finchley Road
  London
  NW3 7BG
  (01-794 5222/8035)

Lesbian Mothers' Group
  c/o Gay Centre
  61A Bloom Street
  Manchester
  M13 LY

Mothers Apart from their Children (MATCH)
  BM Problems
  London
  WC1N 3XX
  (01-892 9949)
Contact: Reg English and Liz Stenning

National Association of Widows,
  c/o Stafford District
  Voluntary Service Centre
  Chell Road
  Stafford
  ST16 2QA
  (0785 45465)

National Coordinating Committee for Parents Under Stress
  29 Newmarket Way
  Hornchurch
  Essex
  (Contact no. 0602 819423)
Contact: Carole Baisden, Sec.

National Council for the Divorced and Separated (NCDS)
  13 High Street
  Little Shelford
  Cambridge
  CB2 5ES
Has branches throughout the country where members can meet on a social
basis or get advice and help with problems.

National Council for One Parent Families
  255 Kentish Town Road
  London
  NW5 2LX
  (01-267 1361)
A national charity set up to help and advise single parents on legal and
welfare rights, housing, tax, childcare and employment, as well as emotional
problems.

National Council for Saturday Parents
  Elfrida Hall
  Campshill Road
  Lewisham
  London
  SE13 6QU
  (01-852 7123, mornings only)

National Marriage Guidance Council
  Herbert Grey College
  Little Church Street
  Rugby
  CV21 3AP
  (0788 73241)
See local telephone directory for nearest branch.

Protestant Adoption Society and Single Parent Counselling Service
  71 Brighton Road
  Rathgar
  Dublin 6
  (0001 972659)

Rights of Women
  374 Gray's Inn Road
  London WC1
  (01-278 6349)
Offers advice on financial, benefit and legal problems, and publishes useful booklets.

Scottish Council for Single Parents
  44 Albany Street
  Edinburgh
  EH1 3QR
  (031-556 3899)
Also at:
  39 Hope Street
  Glasgow
  (041-221 1681)
Help single parents and their families and act as coordinating body and pressure group.

Singlehanded Ltd
  Thorne House
  Hankham Place
  Stone Cross
  Pevensey
  E. Sussex
  BN24 5ER
  (0323 767507)

Appendix 1

Women's Aid Federation England
  374 Gray's Inn Road
  London WC1
  (01-837 9316)
Also at:
  Northern and Publications Office,
  Manchester Women's Centre,
  Manchester
  (061-228 1069)
Help and advice for battered or sexually abused women and their children.

APPENDIX 2

Recommended Reading

Brown, Rosemary, *Breaking Up: A Practical Guide to Separation and Divorce*, Arrow, 1980
Packed with useful information and practical advice.

Clark, Clara, *Coping Alone*, Arlen House, The Women's Press, 1982
Specifically directed at women living in Eire and Northern Ireland and produced as a cooperative venture; includes detailed legal and practical advice and useful addresses.

Coote, Anna, and Gill, Tess, *Women's Rights: A Practical Guide*, Penguin, 1981
Invaluable source of advice on legal, financial, housing and welfare problems.

Davenport, Diana, *One Parent Families*, Sheldon Press, 1979
A helpful manual for single parents, with a very useful list of addresses.

Dineen, Jacqueline, *Going Solo: Starting Out Again After Separation*, Unwin Paperbacks, 1982
Discusses, in a readable way, the emotional and practical consequences of splitting up.

Gatley, Richard, and Konlack, David, *Single Father's Handbook*, Anchor Books, 1979
Although written for American parents, the authors explore the feelings of all those involved very perceptively. The suggestions on food are an insight into eating habits on the other side of the Atlantic!

Hanck, Paul, *Making Marriage Work*, Sheldon Press, 1977
Worth consulting if you are considering splitting up or are worried about

your marriage. Straightforward, matter-of-fact approach to marriage as a working partnership.

Harper, William, *Divorce and Your Money*, Unwin Paperbacks, 1981
Useful source of practical advice on financial matters.

Hooper, Anne, *Divorce and Your Children*, Unwin Paperbacks, 1983
The chapter on children's questions is excellent and certainly worth consulting before talking to your children about what is happening.

Maddox, Brenda, *Stepparenting*, Unwin Paperbacks, 1980
Excellent handbook for those contemplating remarriage or concerned about step-relationships in their family.

Mitchell, Ann, *When Parents Split Up: Divorce Explained to Young People*, Macdonald, 1982
A useful means of working out what you will say to your children, which could also be given to older children to read for themselves.

Rowlands, Peter, *Saturday Parent*, Allen & Unwin, 1980
Considers many of the problems and preoccupations of non-custodial parents and includes a great deal of detailed advice and suggestions.

Search, Gay, *Surviving Divorce: a Handbook for Men*, Elm Tree Books, 1983
As the title suggests, considers divorce from a man's point of view, pointing out their particular problems and difficulties. Sensitive and sympathetic advice.

Wallerstein, Judith, and Kelly, Joan, *Surviving the Breakup*, Grant McIntyre, 1980
A much-quoted study of the effects of divorce on children. Although it offers many insights into children's experience in divorce, it needs to be read with caution as its findings are drawn from an extremely affluent section of American society.

Wolff, Sula, *Children under Stress*, Penguin, 1973
Although not specifically concerned with the stress of parental divorce, the author describes the feelings and experiences of children in stressful situations in a way which many parents will find helpful and reassuring.

NOTES

1. Wallerstein, Judith S., and Kelly, Joan B., *Surviving the Breakup*, Grant McIntyre, 1980, p. 11.
2. See Burgoyne, Jacqueline, and Clark, David, 'Starting Again: Problems and Expectations in Remarriage', *Marriage Guidance*, September 1981.
3. See Leonard, Diana, 'A Proper Wedding', in Corbin, Marie, *Couples*, Penguin Books, 1981; Leonard, Diana, *Sex and Generation*, Tavistock Publications, 1980.
4. Clulow, Christopher, 'Children – For Better, For Worse?' in *Change in Marriage*, National Marriage Guidance Council, 1982; Clulow, Christopher, *To Have and To Hold: Marriage, the First Baby and Preparing Couples for Parenthood*, Aberdeen University Press, 1982.
5. Brown, George, and Harris, Tyrill, *The Social Origins of Depression*, Tavistock Publications, 1980.
6. Nicholson, John, *Seven Ages of Man*, Fontana, 1980.
7. Evans, Paul, and Bartolomé, Fernando, *Must Success Cost So Much?*, Grant McIntyre, 1980, p. 150.
8. ibid., p. 178.
9. *Guardian*, 16 August 1982.
10. Alvarez, A., *Life after Marriage*, Macmillan, 1982, p. 51.
11. Parkes, Colin Murray, *Bereavement: Studies of Grief in Adult Life*, Penguin Books, 1975, p. 20.
12. Alvarez, A., op. cit., p. 53.
13. Newson, John and Elizabeth, *Seven Years Old in the Home Environment*, Penguin Books, 1976.
14. Oakley, Ann, *Becoming a Mother*, Martin Robertson, 1979.
15. George, Victor, and Wilding, P., *Motherless Families*, Routledge & Kegan Paul, 1972.
16. Eekelaar, John, and Clive, Eric, *Custody After Divorce*, Centre for Socio-Legal Studies, 1977.
17. Jackson, Brian, 'Single Parent Families', in Rapoport and others, *Families in Britain*, Routledge, 1982.

18. *Family Finances*, Study Commission on the Family, 1981.
19. Eekelaar and Clive, op. cit.
20. Gibran, Kahlil, *The Prophet*, Heinemann, 1926.
21. See, for example, Maddox, Brenda, *The Half Parent*, André Deutsch, 1975.
22. Wallerstein and Kelly, op. cit., p. 239.
23. Gibran, op. cit.

MORE ABOUT PENGUINS, PELICANS
AND PUFFINS

For further information about books available from Penguins please write to Dept EP, Penguin Books Ltd, Harmondsworth, Middlesex UB7 0DA.

In the U.S.A.: For a complete list of books available from Penguins in the United States write to Dept DG, Penguin Books, 299 Murray Hill Parkway, East Rutherford, New Jersey 07073.

In Canada: For a complete list of books available from Penguins in Canada write to Penguin Books Canada Ltd, 2801 John Street, Markham, Ontario L3R 1B4.

In Australia: For a complete list of books available from Penguins in Australia write to the Marketing Department, Penguin Books Australia Ltd, P.O. Box 257, Ringwood, Victoria 3134.

In New Zealand: For a complete list of books available from Penguins in New Zealand write to the Marketing Department, Penguin Books (N.Z.) Ltd, P.O. Box 4019, Auckland 10.

In India: For a complete list of books available from Penguins in India write to Penguin Overseas Ltd, 706 Eros Apartments, 56 Nehru Place, New Delhi 110019.

WOMEN'S RIGHTS IN THE WORKPLACE

Tess Gill and Larry Whitty

Women and training * Working part-time * Maternity rights *
Women and new technology * Paid work at home * Women
and employment law * Creches and child-care at work

Whether you're employed in an office, a factory or a school,
Women's Rights in the Workplace is designed to arm you with
the information – and the expertise and confidence – to get a
better deal at work. Containing full, up-to-date information
on women's jobs, pay and conditions, it is the essential handbook for all working women.

YOUR SOCIAL SECURITY

Fran Bennett

School-leavers and social security * Benefit and one-parent
families * Retirement pensions * Family income supplement

In practical question and answer format, here at last is a
handbook to guide you through the maze of social security
benefit regulations. Whether you are out of work, a single
parent, retired, disabled or simply grossly underpaid, this
book will give you the essential information to help you claim
your rights from the State.

Other volumes in this new Penguin series *Know Your Rights:
The Questions and the Answers* cover marital rights and the
rights of ethnic minorities.

HEALTH RIGHTS HANDBOOK
A Guide to Medical Care
Gerry and Carol Stimson

A completely up-to-date guide to the medical facilities available to you in Britain. The authors believe that *your body
belongs to you and only you should decide what to do with it and
what to have done to it*. Their book will help you to understand
the NHS itself and to deal with doctors and other health
workers in order to get the most out of the services available.

OUR BODIES OURSELVES
A Health Book by and for women
Boston Women's Health Book Collective
British Edition by Angela Phillips and Jill Rakusen

The most successful book about women ever published, *Our
Bodies Ourselves* has sold over one million copies worldwide.

'Every woman in the country should be issued with a copy free
of charge' – *Mother and Baby*

'Well researched, informative and educational for both men
and women' – *British Medical Journal*

'The Bible of the woman's health movement' – *Guardian*

'If there's only one book you ever buy – this should be it' – *19*

WHERE CAN I GET ...?

Beryl Downing

Who will repair my luggage, restring my beads, paint a portrait of me or my dog?

Where can I buy a chess set, an antique mirror or a jumper made-to-order?

How can I find an entertainer for my party, a caterer, or a horse and carriage for my wedding?

Find out in this invaluable handbook, compiled by Beryl Downing, writer of the popular Saturday shopping page in *The Times*. Here she proves that personal service and quality goods are *not* things of the past – and arms you with the information to track them down. All the goods and services mentioned – from restoring and hiring to sending unusual gifts by post – have been personally recommended.

THE PENGUIN LONDON MAPGUIDE

The Penguin London Mapguide contains everything you need to know to enjoy yourself and get the best out of London. It includes

- Art Galleries and
    Museums
- Markets
- Underground Stations
- Places of interest

- Theatres and Cinemas
- Parks
- Bus Routes
- Tourist Information
    Centres

and

Detailed plans of the National Gallery, Regent's Park Zoo and the Tower of London.

A Choice of Penguins

THE PENGUIN STEREO RECORD
AND CASSETTE GUIDE 1982

Edward Greenfield, Robert Layton and Ivan March

Following the enormously successful *Penguin Stereo Record Guide* and *Penguin Cassette Guide*, here is a superb, comprehensive and reliable listing and evaluation of the finest stereo records and cassettes currently available in the U.K.

- alphabetical listing by composer
- analysis of technical quality
- comment on character of performance
- reissues of outstanding mono recordings
- information on imports
- bargain records and tapes
- concerts and recitals included

THE PENGUIN GUIDE TO THE LAW

John Pritchard

Written and designed for everyday use in everyday life, *The Penguin Guide to the Law* is the most comprehensive handbook to the law as it affects the individual ever compiled. In it you can find out about the legal aspects of family matters, housing, employment, consumer affairs, small businesses, motoring, civil liberties and social security. Laid out clearly and logically it is the definitive manual for the home and office and will enable those daunted by the complexity of the law to understand and solve the ever more intricate problems of the day.

BUYING A HOUSE OR FLAT

Second Edition

L. E. Vickers

Previously published as *Buying a House*, *Buying a House or Flat* is a concise, comprehensive and up-to-date account of how to acquire your own property.

All the details required are here – the financial and the legal, the building societies, the estate agents, solicitors and surveyors. Methodically Mrs Vickers outlines the various ways of raising money and the intricacies of conveyance and explains the force (or weakness) of a deposit, the meaning of 'freehold' and 'leasehold' and the rights of sitting tenants. On a less legal level she urges caution about the winter aspect of houses viewed in summer and other pitfalls, and reminds purchasers of all the arrangements to be made for moving day.

Those embarking on the exciting process of acquiring a new home could have no better guide: for the author, as well as having a sense of humour, has a flourishing practice as a solicitor.

SELF HELP HOUSE REPAIRS MANUAL

New Expanded Edition

Andrew Ingham

This updated and revised edition covers all aspects of basic repairs: electricity – repairing existing installations, putting in a new circuit; water – piping, sinks, baths, lavatories; gas – water heaters, cookers, fires; general repair – roofs, dry rot, plastering. New information on general carpentry, window repairs, draught-proofing, sanding floors and much more.

Cookery in Penguin Handbooks

GERALDENE HOLT'S CAKE STALL

Honey Crunch Tea-Bread, Praline Cream Gâteau, Harvest Cake, Iced Gingerbread, Chocolate Cup Cakes, Easter Biscuits

These are only a selection of the delicious wares that Geraldene Holt sold from her enormously successful cake stall at Tiverton Pannier Market. (Now there are a string of similar cake stalls all over the country.) Collected into this book, her recipes will tempt even the most hard-hearted into action, and her advice on equipment, techniques and useful short cuts to success will ensure that hungry families everywhere are treated to amazing tea-time delights.

JOSCELINE DIMBLEBY'S BOOK OF PUDDINGS, DESSERTS AND SAVOURIES

Puddings to make the family gasp, desserts to amaze a formal gathering, savouries to round off a perfect meal ...

Here Josceline Dimbleby has gathered together a selection of pies, tarts, gâteaux, mousses, cheesecakes, ice-creams and savouries which will inspire even the most jaded cook. Practical, easy and often inspired by the flavours of the Orient, they can be relied on to add a new dimension to your cooking.